Oregon Townscape Walks

by Tyler Burgess

www.Walk-With-Me.com

First edition March 2009

Published by
Walk With Me
1430 Willamette St. #579
Eugene, OR 97401

Printed in Canada
www.Walk-With-Me.com

I have designed and walked all these routes. But as we know, shift happens. Construction and new businesses change the townscape. Corrections are welcome.

Mileage is by gmap-pedometer.com
Base map is ODOT.

Special thanks to Janice Gould and Ruth Romoser for doing research with me.

Other Books by author:
Walking Made Powerful
Eugene, Oregon Walks
How to Walk a Marathon, 26.2 Tips

ISBN 978-0-9816599-1-6

Explore Townscapes by Pedestrian Power

Experience community character imparted by past ghosts and present folks!

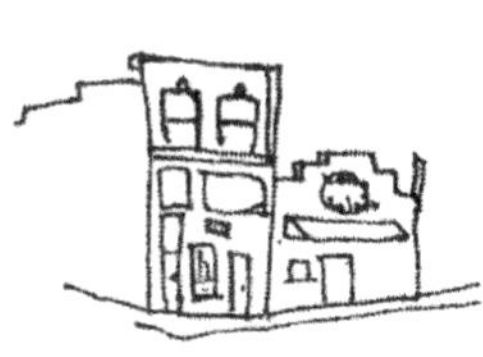

Main Street: Cowboys and gold prospectors once swaggered along here. Gracing the Old West flavor of scenic sites is beautiful new public art.

Spectacular homes sprouted up around whistle stops. Today you can walk from the same depots through a historic neighborhood and perhaps stay at a charming B+B.

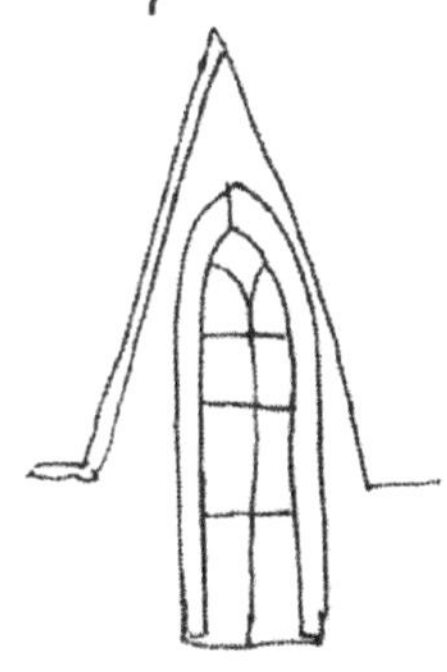

History reveals itself on plaques:

- along the Willamette River,
- at Engine No. 2579 in Klamath Falls,
- the Skevington Crossing in Rogue River.

and many other places.

Tromp through the courthouses, city hall, museums and Capitol in Salem.

Enchanting Walking Routes. These maps organize your walk through a collage of buildings, streets and spaces to affirm the power of the pedestrian and give you a sense of place.

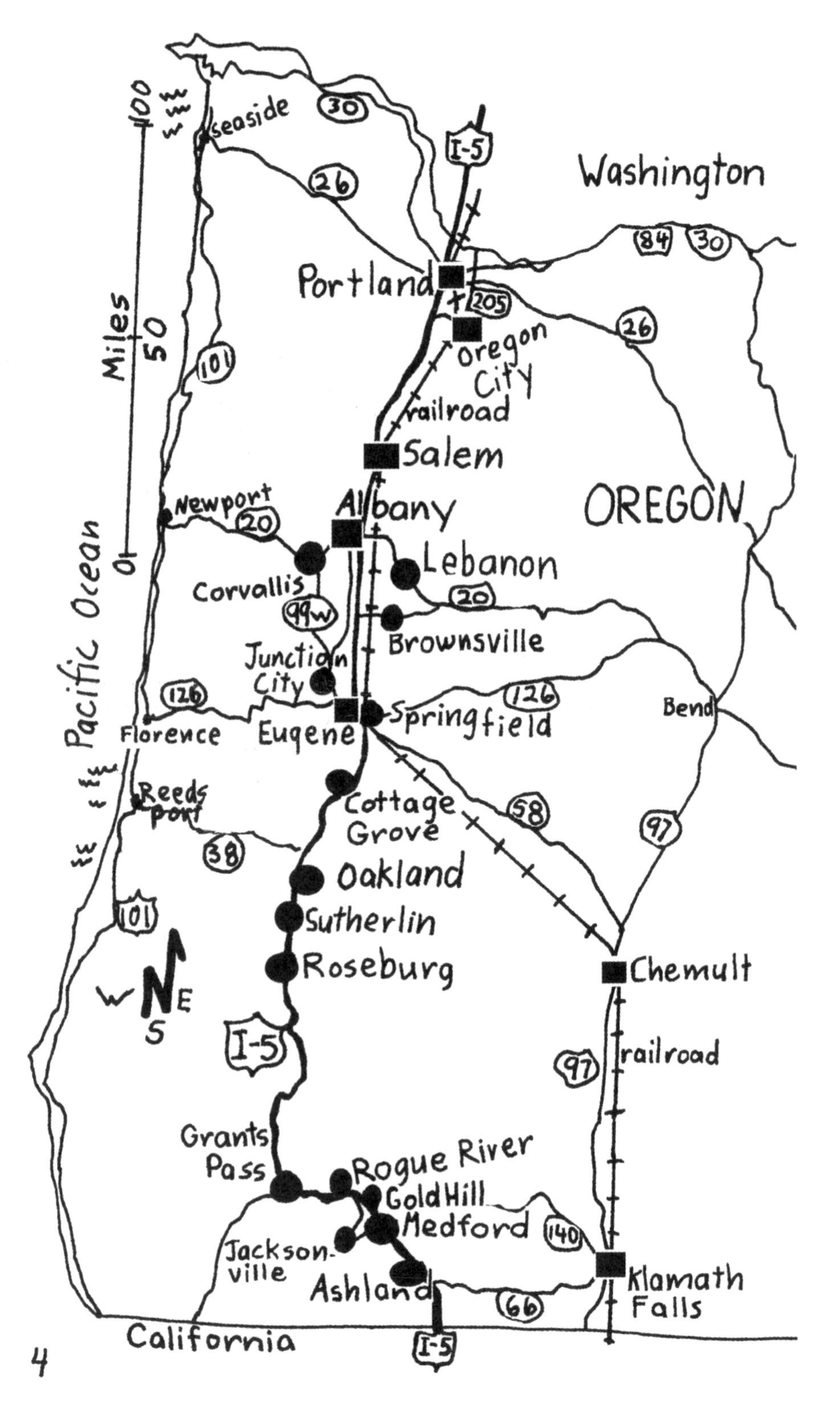

Seaside
30
I-5
Washington
26
84
30
Portland
205
26
Oregon City
railroad
Salem
Miles
100
50
0
101
Newport
20
Albany
OREGON
Lebanon
Corvallis
20
99w
Brownsville
Pacific Ocean
Junction City
126
126
Bend
Florence
Eugene
Springfield
Reeds port
Cottage Grove
58
97
38
Oakland
101
Sutherlin
Roseburg
Chemult
W
E
S
I-5
97
railroad
Grants Pass
Rogue River
Gold Hill
Medford
140
Jacksonville
Ashland
Klamath Falls
66
California
I-5

TABLE of CONTENTS

		Page
Albany	Amazing Albany	8
	Directions	9
	Three Historic Districts	10
	Lodging	11
Ashland	Historic Railroad Area	12
	Skidmore Neighborhood	14
	Lithia Park to OSU	16
Brownsville	Country Charm	18
	Walk in Time	20
	History and Hops	22
Chemult	Hike, cross-country ski	24
Coburg	Charming Coburg	26
Corvallis	Overview	28
	Historic Downtown	30
	Franklin Park, Atomic Homes	32
	College Hill West	34
	OSU Campus	36
	Willamette Park, Cemetery	38
Cottage Grove	Historic Homes	40
	Row River Trail	42
Eugene	Directions, Lodging	44
	Train Depot to UO	46
	Skinner Butte	48
	River Bike Path	50
Gold Hill	Downtown and River	52
Grants Pass	Downtown to Midland	54
	Downtown to River	56
Jacksonville	Downtown	58
	Around Downtown, Cemetery	60
Junction City		62
Klamath Falls	Directions Lodging	64
	OC+E Woods Line	65
	Downtown and Trails	66
	Cemetery, 9 churches	68
Lebanon	Healing Garden	70
	Classic Downtown	72

Medford.. Historic Homes............ 74
Historic Downtown........ 76
Oregon City... Directions, Lodging........... 78
Willamette Falls........... 80
Top Tier Trek.............. 82
River Views............... 84
Portland....... Directions, Lodging........... 86
Historic Irvington Homes.. 88
Parks, PSU, Powells........ 90
Pearl and Pigs on 23rd.. 92
River Loop to OMSI...... 94
Ladd Addition to River... 96
Tram and Trolley.......... 98
Rogue River, City, State Park, Rest Area.. 100
Roseburg... Around Downtown...... 102
Laurelwood Park and River 104
Veterans and River...... 106
Salem...... Directions, Lodging....... 108
Taste of Salem......... 110
Mill to Governor's Mansion 112
Capitol and Creeks....... 114
Springfield.. Directions............. 117
Washburne Historic Area 116
Dorris Ranch............ 118
Kelly Butte.............. 120
Sutherlin.......................... 122

Walker's Diary.......................... 124
About the author...................... 126

Amtrak stop, with walk route and nearby lodging.

Access to a paved bicycle route on this map.

Oregon Townscapes

Discover a walker's wonderland in 22 Oregon townscapes near I-5 highway and from 7 Amtrak stops.

Directions and maps include walking route and lodging close to Amtrak stops. For train reservations: call 1-800-872-7245 online at www.amtrak.com Trains may run late, but patience is rewarded!

Mileage varies, with some routes offering shorter options. Many can be linked as they share a common start point.

BE SAFE! Look both ways before crossing every street. Occasionally, there is no side walk on a street. Walk on the left side, facing traffic.

Legend

- ● Start and finish here.
- ••• shorter option
- → one way traffic
- ⇄ go both ways
- **R** Right
- **L** Left
- **P** Parking
- mi. Mileage
- Hill

F, Food, may be cafe, grocery, deli, coffee shop.

Public restrooms are marked on the maps.

AMAZING ALBANY

Distance: 2.7 mi. flat on sidewalks

Start/finish at Train Station, 110 West 10th St.
Free car parking.
Walk down to clock tower.
L across street, on left side.
Under bridge. First **R** at light, to median island.
L across Lyon. **R** on Lyon, 1 block

L on 8th, Victorian Gazebo+Garden
At dead end, **L** on Washington
R on 10th, 1 block.
R on Calapooia.
L on 7th Av. SW

R on Elm, 1 block
R on 6th Av.
L on Calapooia, 2 blocks
R on 4th Av, 2 blocks
L on Ferry, library has public restrooms downstairs.
R on 1st St, 1 block.

R on Broadalbin.
L on sidewalk next to courthouse.
follow walk around building.
Continue on Broadalbin.

L on 7th Av.
R on Railroad St. across parking lot.
R on path.
L under bridge to train station.

Directions from I-5 to start at Amtrak Station.

From the North, Exit 234B.
Follow signs to Albany.
Merge onto 99E / Pacific Blvd.
L on 12th, straight to roundabout.

From the south, Exit 228.
Go toward Corvallis on OR 34.
R on 99E/sw Pacific Blvd.
R at 12th St. to roundabout.

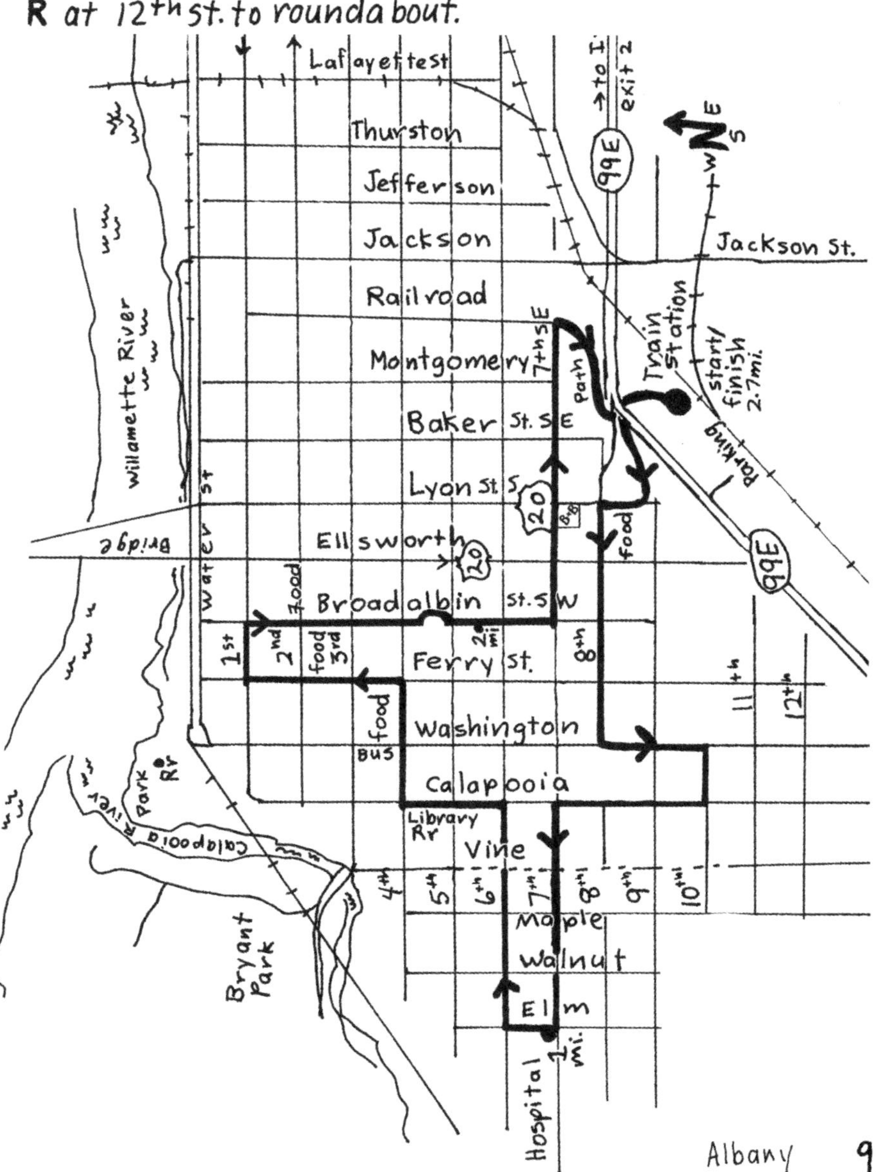

THREE HISTORIC DISTRICTS

ALBANY

Distances: 2 mi. Use ••• on map to shorten route.
4 mi. flat on sidewalks

Start/finish at train Station, 110 West 10th St.
Walk to clock tower.
L under bridge, on left hand side.
At first corner, **L** on 9th Av.
L on Ferry, 2 blocks. **R** on 12th, 1 block.
R on Washington.

L on 9th Av.
R on Maple, 1 block.
L on 8th one block.
R on Walnut
R on 5th
L on Washington

Straight into Monteith Park.
Cross parking lot, go to river.
R on path along river, pass restrooms.
Continue under bridge.
R across tracks at crossing.
L on street (Water St.) 1 block.

R on Montgomery, 1 block.
L on 1st. **L** on Ferry 1 block.
L on 2nd Av. **R** on Lyon, 1 block.
L on 3rd Av.
R on Thurston Creek, 2 blocks.

R on 5th Av. **L** on Montgomery, 2 blocks.
R on 7th **L** on Ellsworth. Cross 9th Av.
L on 9th. **R** under bridge to Station.

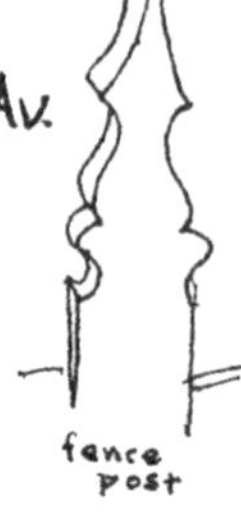

Lodging near train station: From Amtrak depot, walk downhill to clock tower. **L** across street. Under bridge. First right to traffic island. Cross Lyon st. and go **R** one block. to:

Train House B+B, 1-541-791-5281
206 7th Ave. SW

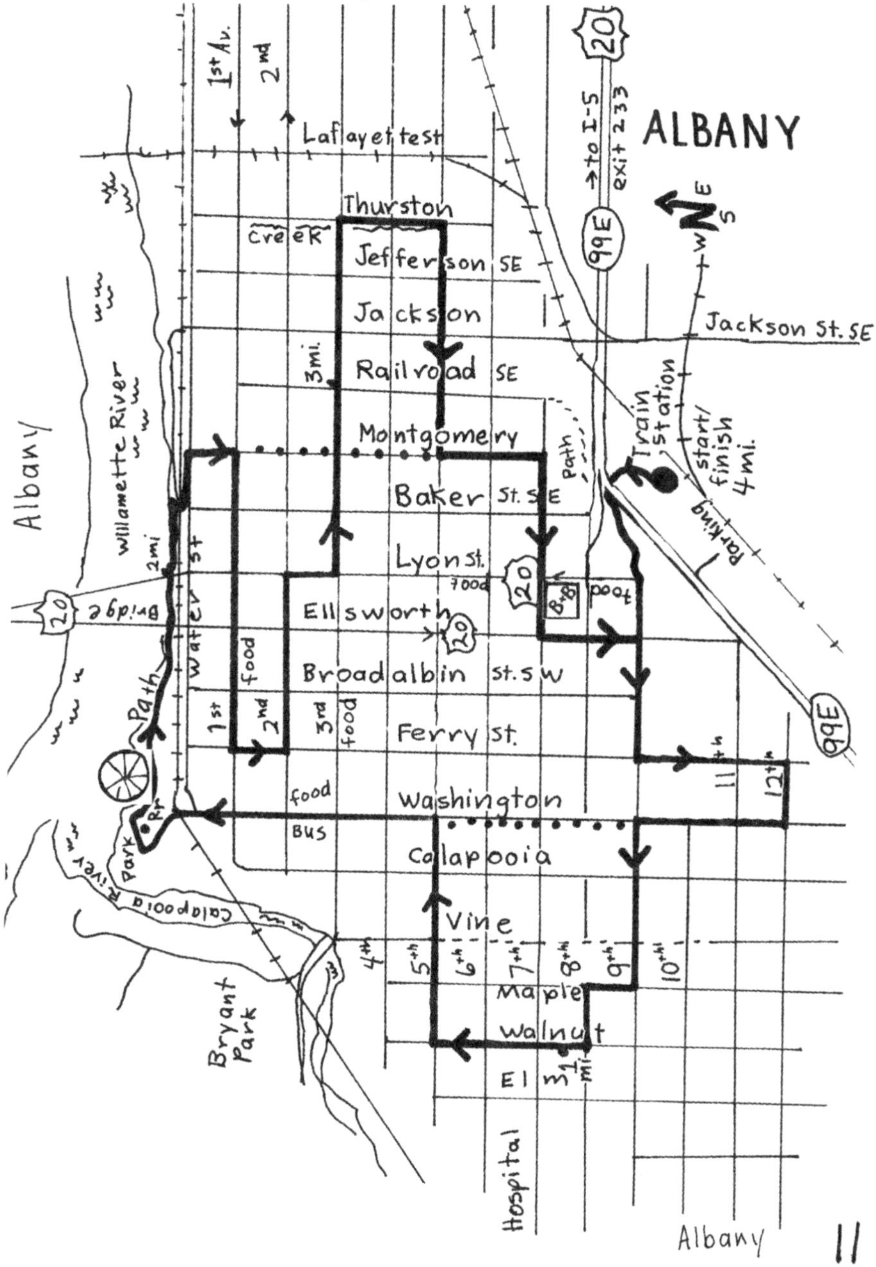

HISTORIC RAILROAD Area

Ashland

Distance: 2.5 miles, flat.

130 4th St

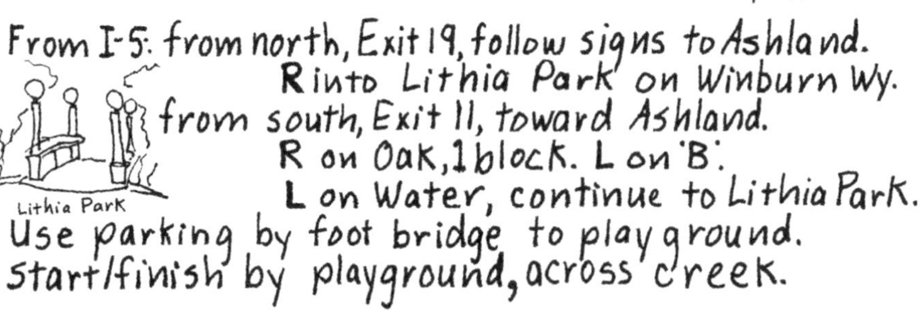

From I-5: from north, Exit 19, follow signs to Ashland.
R into Lithia Park on Winburn Wy.
from south, Exit 11, toward Ashland.
R on Oak, 1 block. **L** on 'B'.
L on Water, continue to Lithia Park.
Use parking by foot bridge to playground.
Start/finish by playground, across creek.

Take the downhill path. The creek is on your left.
R at street (Winburn), 1 block.
R on E. Main. Cross to left side.

Cross 8th. Go **L**.
L on 'A', 1 block. **L** on 7th.
R on 'C', 1 block. **R** on 6th.
L on 'A', 1 block. **L** on 5th.
R on 'C', 1 block. **R** on 4th.

L on 'A', 1 block.
L on 3rd, 1 block.
R on 'B'.
R on Pioneer St.
L on 'A', 1 block.

L on Oak. **R** at end.
Cross E. Main. **L** at corner.
Through park on path to end.

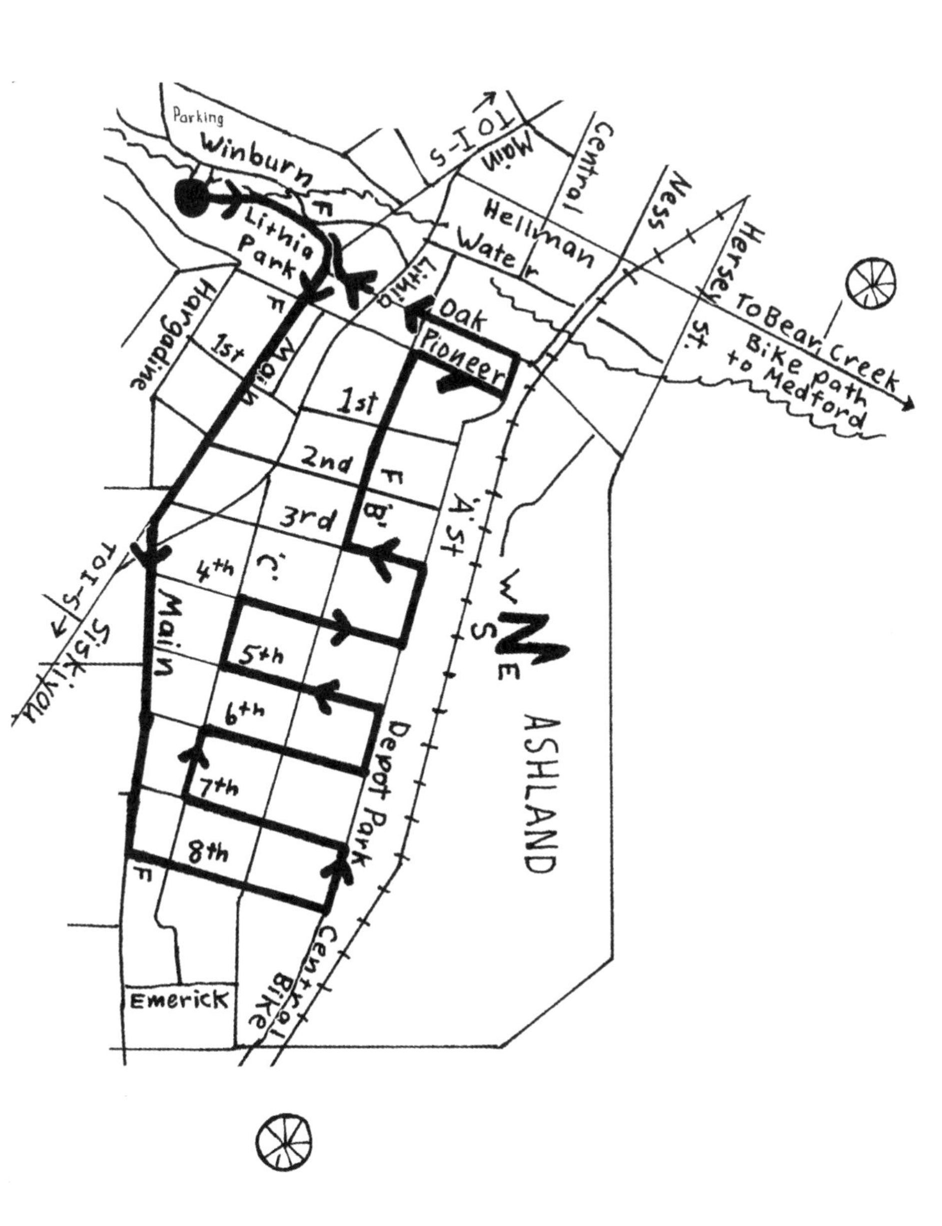

Parking
Winburn
Lithia Park
TO I-5
Main
Central
Ness
Hersey St.
Hellman
Water
Lithia
Oak
Pioneer
Hargadine
1st
Main
1st
2nd
3rd
'B'
'C'
'A' St
4th
5th
6th
7th
8th
F
Main
Siskiyou
TO I-5
Depot Park
Central Bike
Emerick
To Bear Creek
Bike path to Medford
N
S
E
W
ASHLAND

SKIDMORE Historic Area
Ashland

Distance: 1.1mi., 2.2mi., or 3mi. Ascent 72ft.

From I-5: from north, Exit 19, follow signs to Ashland.
R into Lithia Park on Winburn Wy.
from south, Exit 11, toward Ashland.
R on Oak, 1 block. **L** on 'B'.
L on Water, continue to Lithia Park.

Lithia Park

Use parking by foot bridge to playground.
Start/finish by playground, across creek.

Take uphill path, with creek on your right.
R at picnic tables to cross bridge.
L at street. Curve **L** to path.
Cross parking lot.
Cross Granite St, go **R**.
(for 1mi, **R** on Nutley to Lithia Park)

L on Baum, becomes unpaved and Almond St.
R on Manzanita, 1 block.
R on High st.

cute house award

203 High

L on Church, 1 block. (for 2mi, **R** on Main. See * below)
L to traffic light →
R across to Helman.
L on Van Ness.
L on No. Main.

R at Helman, across Main, then go **L** 1 block.
*Cross Granite, before the bridge, go **R** on path.
Pass rest rooms.
R at street (Winburn) to end.

94 Granite

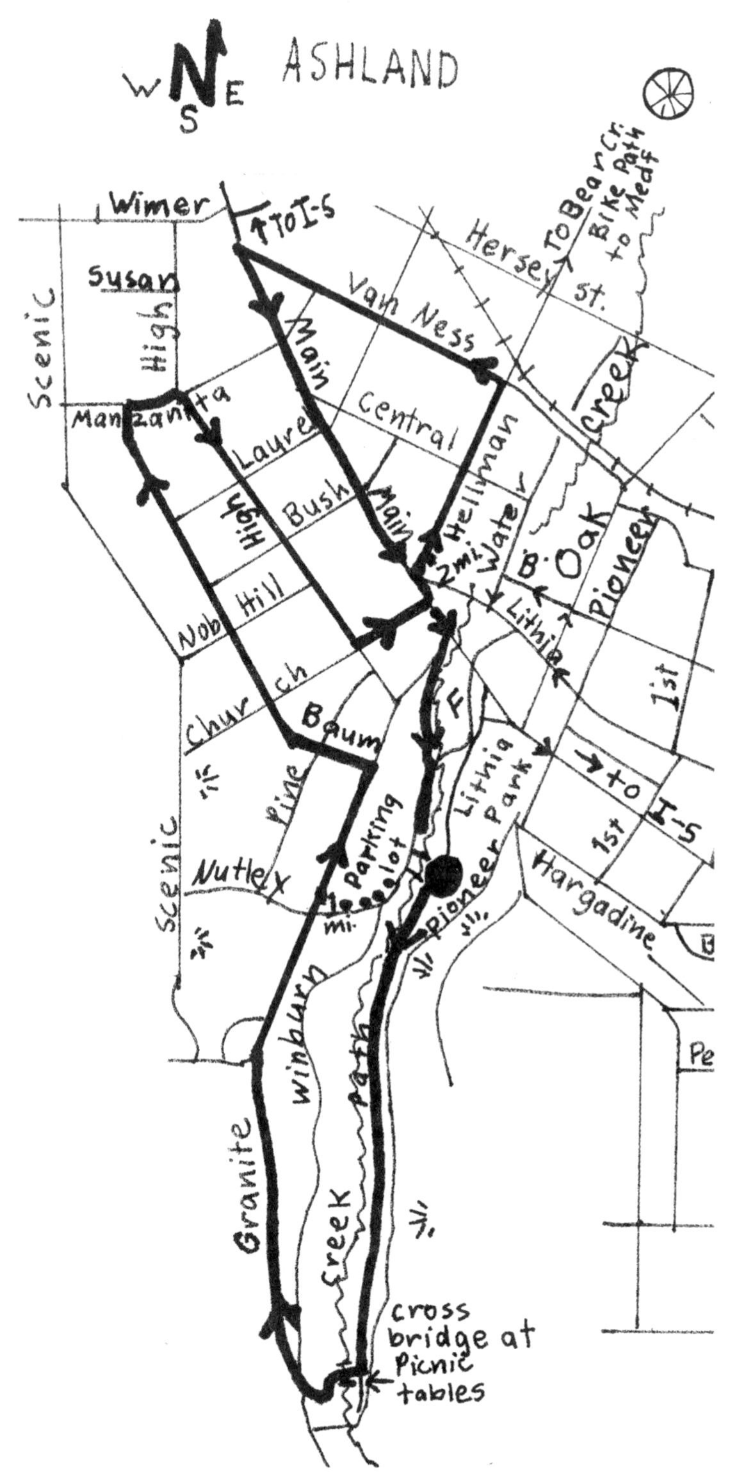
ASHLAND
N
W
E
S
Wimer
TO I-5
Susan
Scenic
High
Van Ness
Hersey St.
To Bear Cr. Bike Path to Medf
Creek
Main
Manzanita
Laurel
Central
Hellman
Bush
Main
High
2 mi.
Water
B
Oak
Pioneer
Hill
Nob
Lithia
Church
1st
F
Baum
Lithia Park
to I-5
Pine
Parking lot
Scenic
Nutley
1 mi.
Pioneer
1st
Hargadine
Winburn
Path
Granite
Creek
cross bridge at Picnic tables

LITHIA PARK to SOU campus

Ashland

Distances: 1.7 mi., 3 mi., 4 mi. Ascent 85 ft.

Start/finish: Playground at Lithia Park.
See directions on other Ashland maps.
Your back to the playground, go **L** around restrooms. **L** down path.
L at fork. **R** around pond.
R at main path. Emerge on Winburn.
L to corner.

Pond in Lithia Park.

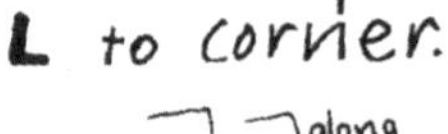

R across street to Calle Guanjuato, path along creek. At street (Main), jog **L** then **R** to cross. Down steps along creek. **L** at parking lot. Pass the Day Spa. **R** along creek. **R** at street (Water).

L on Main. At 2nd st, cross to walk on **R** side.
(for 1.7 mi. option, **R** on Union, **R** on Fairview. See ✱)
(for 3 mi., **R** on Mountain, **R** on Henry. See ▲).
R on Indiana. **R** up steps to S. Homes Res. Hall.
R at fork. Pass Hannon Library.
R on diagonal path, past bell tower.
L past Bookstore. Cross next street (University), on path behind Edu./Psyc. Building.

Cross Mountain. Straight on Henry.
▲ Cross Liberty, go **R**, 1 block.
L on Penn. 1 block. **R** down Morton.
L on Holly. **R** on Idaho, 1 block.

R on Iowa, 1 block. **L** on Fairview.
✱ Cross Gresham, go **R**.
L on Hargadine, curves **R**.
At end, cross street (Pioneer)
Veer **L**, down steps. **L** to end.

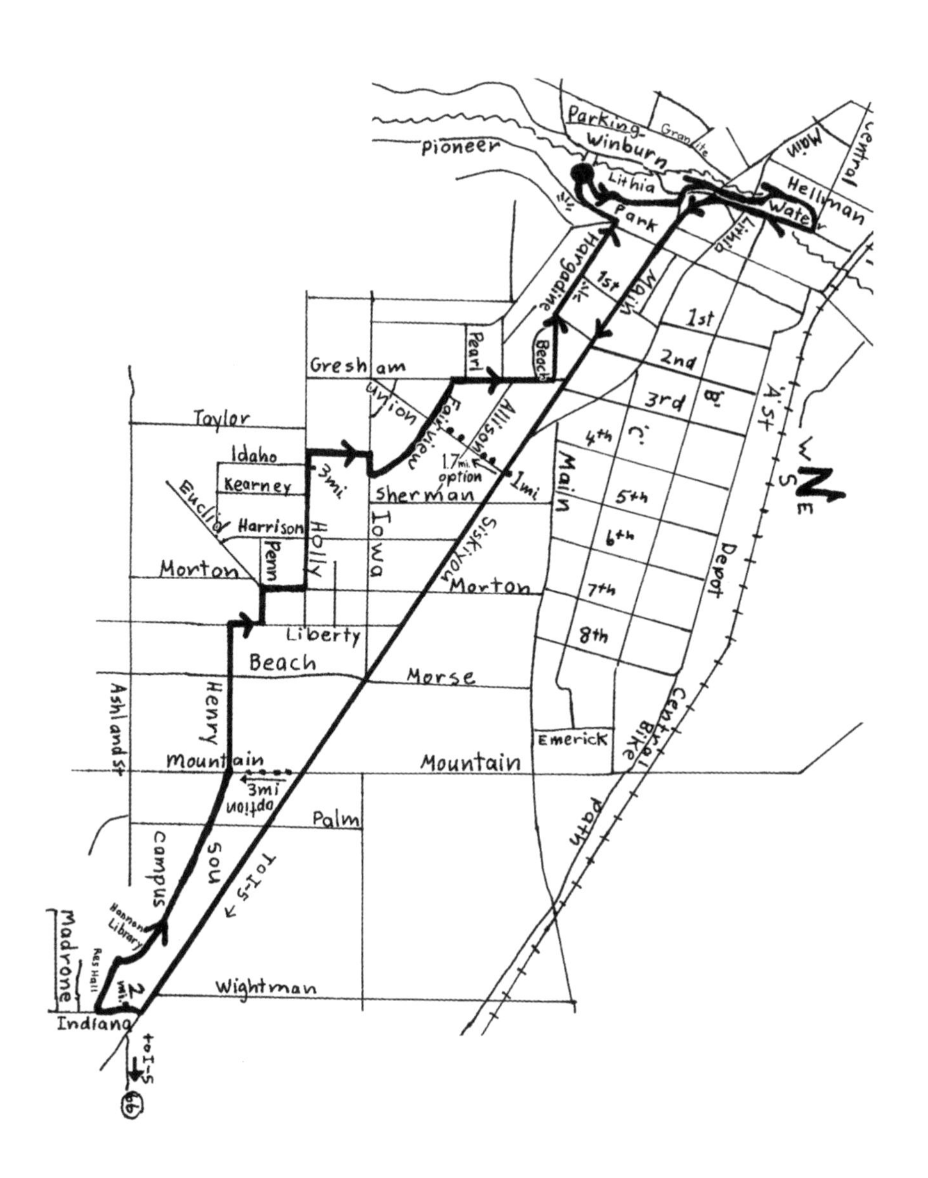
Parking-
Granite
Main
Central
Pioneer
Winburn
Lithia
Hellman
Water
Park
Lithia
Hargadine
1st
Main
1st
2nd
3rd
'B'
'A' St
Pearl
Beach
Gresham
Union
Fairview
Allison
Taylor
Idaho
Kearney
3mi
1.7mi. option
1mi
Sherman
4th
'C'
Main
5th
6th
Euclid
Harrison
Penn
Holly
Iowa
Siskiyou
Morton
Morton
7th
Depot
8th
Liberty
Beach
Morse
Henry
Ashland st
Mountain
Mountain
Emerick
Central Bike path
3mi option
Palm
Campus
Sou
To I-5
Madrone
Hannon Library
Res Hall
2 mi.
Wightman
Indiana
to I-5
66

BROWNSVILLE

Directions: from I-5, north or south bound.
Take exit 216 to Sweethome Highway.
L on Main St.
R on Park Av., 1/2 block to museum.
Free parking on street.

COUNTRY CHARM

Distance: 2.6 miles, flat.

Start/finish: Linn Co. Historical Museum, 101 Park Ave.

Face the museum.
Go **L** on Park Av.
Cross Main St. Go **L**
After bridge, **R** on Vroman.
L at street (Washburn).
L on Blakely.

Spire from washington st.

Pear tree

R on Templeton.
L on Kisling, 1 block.
L on Rose, 1 block.
L on Cooley, 1 block.

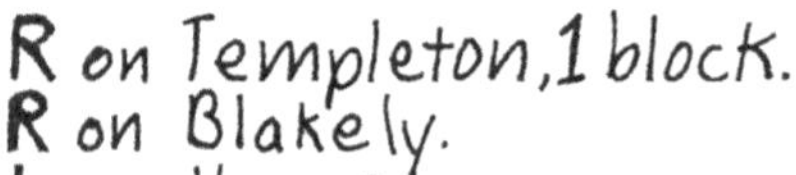

R on Templeton, 1 block.
R on Blakely.
L on Hume.
L on Washington.
L on Faust.
R on Blakely.

on Cooley

R on Rose.
L on Washington.

holly leaf

Robe St.

R on Washburn.
L at street (Main).
R on Park Av.

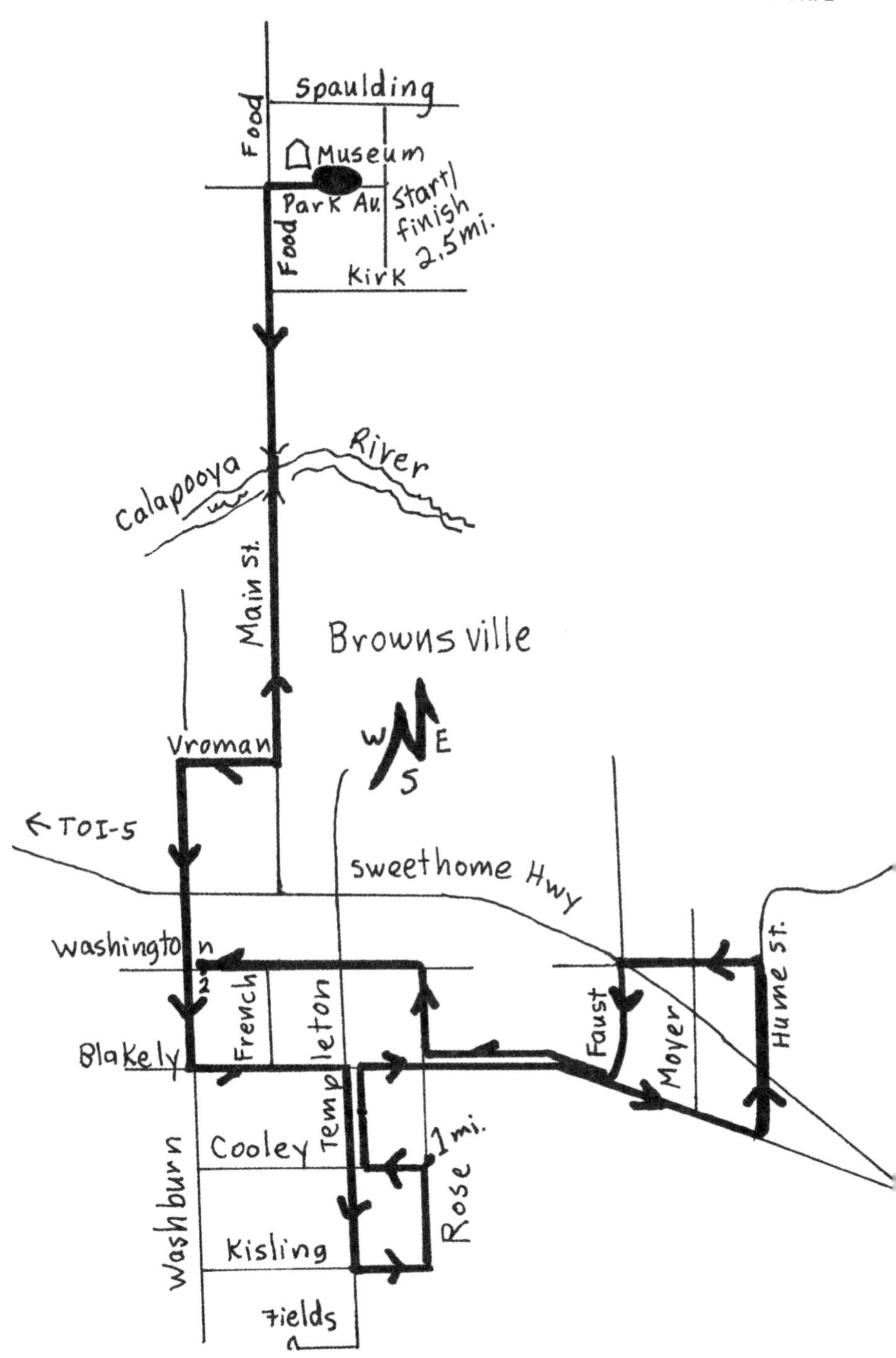
Spaulding
Food
Museum
Park Av.
Start/
finish
2.5mi.
Food
Kirk
Calapooya
River
Main St.
Brownsville
Vroman
W
E
S
← TO I-5
sweethome Hwy
washington
2
French
Templeton
Blakely
Faust
Moyer
Hume St.
Cooley
1mi.
Rose
Washburn
Kisling
Fields

WALK IN TIME

The short version of "History and Hops"!

The museum has a free history brochure.

Distance: 1.6 miles, flat

Start/finish: Linn Co. Historical Museum, 101 Park Av.

Face the museum.
R to path beside boxcar.
L on Menefee Walkway.
L at street (Spaulding).
Cross Main St. go **L**, 1 block.
Cross next street (Park Av)
go **R** on Park Av.

LIBRARY
food shops
millrace
start
Park St

on Ash

Ben Fisher's tool shed for his sawmill.

R on Fisher.
R on Walnut 1 block.
L on Ash 1 block.
R on Locust 1 block. **L** on Oak.

Cross Depot Av. go **L** 1 block.
R on Ash 1 block.
L on Coshow 1 block.
R on Pine.

R on Hausman. **R** on Oak.
L on Depot.
R on Main St. Curves **L** on Standard
R on Averill.
R on Park Av. to finish.

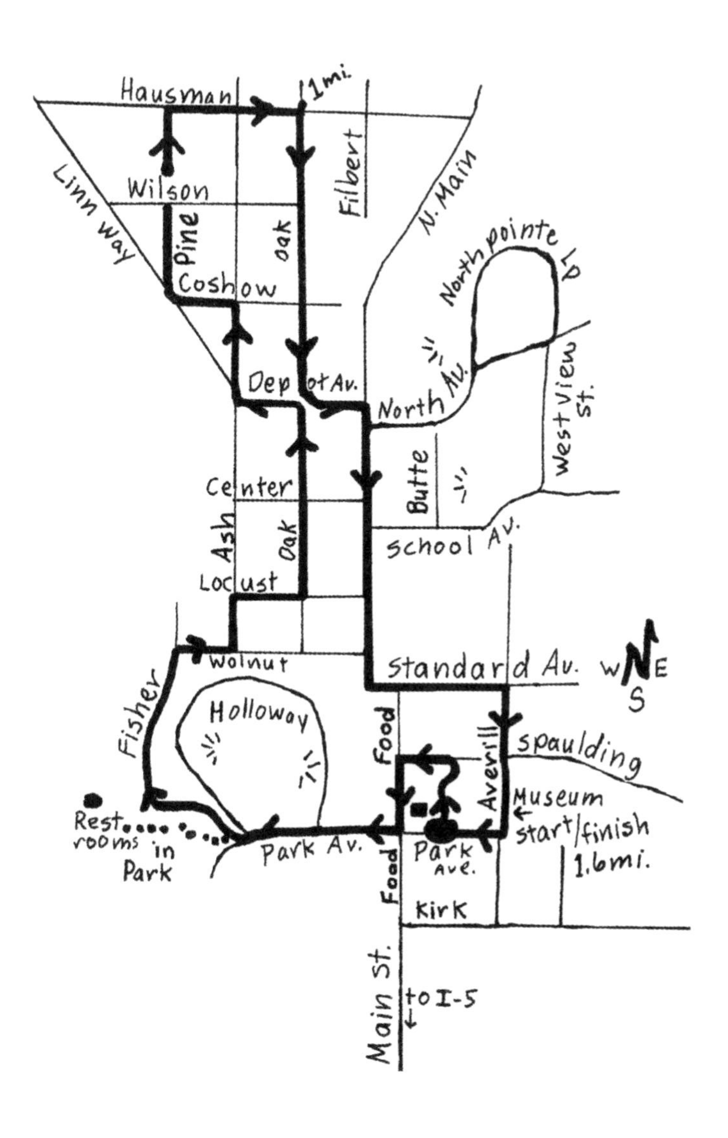
Hausman
1mi.
Filbert
N. Main
Linn Way
Wilson
Pine
Oak
Coshow
Northpointe Lp
North Av.
West View St.
Depot Av.
North
Butte
Center
Ash
Oak
School Av.
Locust
Walnut
Standard Av.
W N E S
Fisher
Holloway
Food
Averill
Spaulding
Museum
start/finish
1.6mi.
Rest rooms in Park
Park Av.
Park Ave.
Food
Kirk
Main St.
to I-5

HISTORY and HOPS

Distance: 3.2 mi. flat, or 6.3 mi. elevation 250 ft.

Start/finish: Linn Co. Historical Museum
Face the museum.
R to path beside boxcar.
L on Menefee Walkway.
L at street (Spaulding)
Cross Main St., go **L**, 1 block.
Cross street (Park) go **R**.

R up Halloway Hts before park
R after this loop, onto Park St.
straight into city park.
L through parking lot. **L** on path.
Curves **R**, (toilets).

Exit park. **L** on Fisher.
R on Walnut, 1 block. **L** on Ash, 1 block
R on Locust, 1 block. **L** on Oak.

Cross Depot Av.
L on Depot, 1 block. **R** on Ash 1 block.
L on Coshow, 1 block. **R** on Pine.
R on Hausman. **R** on Oak.
L on Depot. Cross Main, go **R**.
Immediate **L** up North Av.,
curves **R**. **R** down North Av.

Cross Main St. go **L**. Curves **L** to Standard St
R on Averill, 1 block. **L** on Spaulding.
L on Kirk. **L** on Putman. **R** on Spaulding.
R at corner (downhill). **L** at T, curves **R**.
L on Weber. **R** at T **L** on Kirk. (3.2 mi, see *)
Straight on road. Curves
up to Pioneer cemetery
Return on Left hand (toilet)
side. **L** on Hunter. (3.2 mi. *)
R on Calapooia. **R** on Putman.
L on Kirk. **R** on Averill.
L on Park Av.

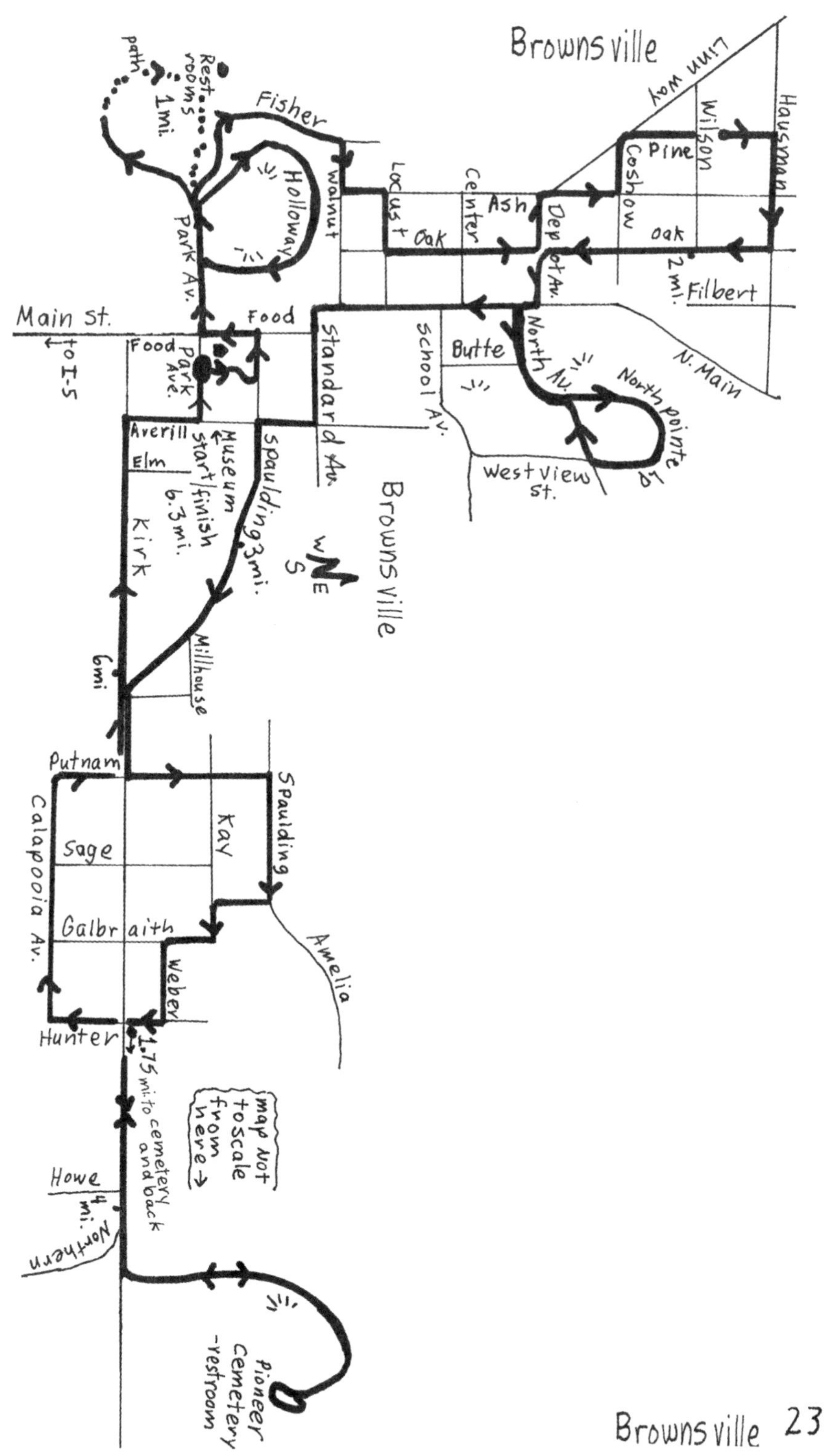
Brownsville
Linn Way
Hausman
Wilson
Pine
Coshow
Oak
Ash
Depot Av.
Center
Locust
Oak
Walnut
Fisher
Holloway
Rest rooms
path
1mi.
Park Av.
2mi.
Filbert
N. Main
Main St.
to I-5
Food
Food
Park Ave.
Standard Av.
School Av.
Butte
North Av.
North Pointe Dr
Westview St.
Averill
Elm
Museum start/finish 6.3mi.
Spaulding 3mi.
Kirk
Brownsville
W N E S
Millhouse
6mi
Putnam
Calapooia Av.
Sage
Kay
Spaulding
Galbraith
Amelia
Weber
Hunter
1.75 mi. to cemetery and back
map not to scale from here →
Howe
4 mi.
Northern
Pioneer Cemetery -restroom

CHEMULT Hike, Cross-country ski

Amtrak stops here, along Hwy 97 N.
In winter, the street may be
icy at the Amtrak stop!

Walk or ski to the Ranger Station.
Cross busy Hwy 97.
R along road, or ski under
the powerline.

Maps available 24/7 at the
entry of the Ranger Station.
Both ski and hiking maps
are available.
Ranger Station, 541-305-7001.

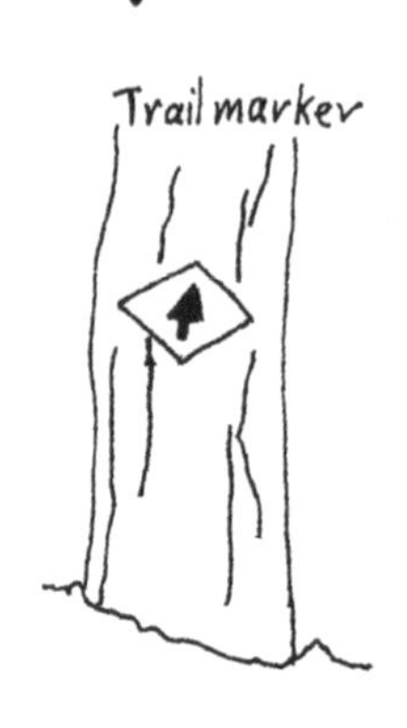

To Walt Harding Park from
Ranger Station, on foot:
Walk behind Ranger Station
to the STOP sign.
Veer right, then left through
the work area to the
trail leading uphill.
R at the first intersection, into
the Park. Restrooms, picnic
tables, 5 campsites, water.

<u>Driving</u>; turn off 97N at Walt Harding
Sno Park. This is the site of the
high school cross-country championship ski.
Dog sled races are here late January.

<u>Lodging</u>: Dawson House Lodge.
1 block from Amtrak, on Hwy 97.
1-888-281-8375.

Area shuttle, 541-365-2394, to
see Crater Lake, summer only.

Crater
Lake

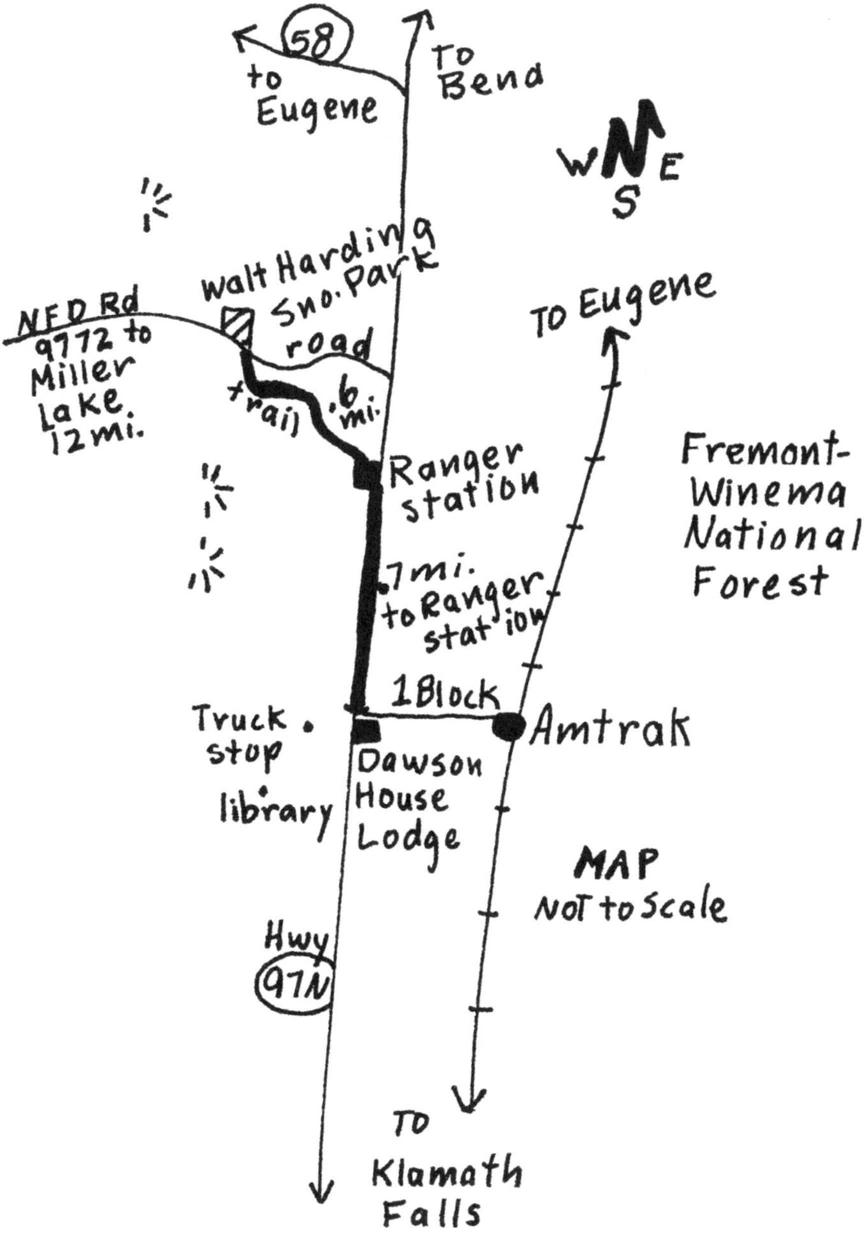

58
to Eugene
To Bend
W N E S
Walt Harding Sno.Park road
NFD Rd 9772 to Miller Lake. 12mi.
trail
.6 mi.
Ranger station
.7mi. to Ranger station
TO Eugene
Fremont-Winema National Forest
1Block
Truck stop
Amtrak
Dawson House Lodge
library
MAP
Not to Scale
Hwy 97N
TO Klamath Falls

CHARMING COBURG

end of Christian Way

Distances: 3 mi. flat or 5.5 mi. flat

On I-5 take exit 199 to Coburg.
L on Harrison, ½ block to free parking lot.
Walk back to Pearl. **L** on Pearl. Cross Pearl to kiosk for brochure "Coburg Historic Homes."

32801 Maple
Farm Bungalow

Cross Willamette St. go **L**.
R on Christian Way to end, return.
Cross Willamette St. Go **L** to corner.
R on Dixon. **R** on Skinner.
Curves into Maple. At house 32081, return to Coleman.

R on Coleman. **L** on Dixon.
R on Skinner. **R** on Delaney.
L on Miller. At house 91212, return.

Cute House Award
32648 Van Duyn

R on Mill. **L** on Skinner.
R on McKenzie. **R** on Diamond.
(Restrooms in park.)
L on Locust. **R** on Harrison 1 block.
L on Van Duyn St.
L on Willamette 50 ft.
R to Cross Willamette to Bruce St.

Canterbury Slough

Beyond red fire hydrant at Bruce and Water, follow faint trail. Curves **L** then **R** behind houses. Behind last house, **L** to Nature trail. (3 mi. option).

for 5.5 mi. **R** on path to road. **L** on road to end. Return to path (at ⑨ sign). Take Nature trail.
R on Street. **R** on Abbey.
Take path **L** of 91050 Abbey.
L on Street (Water). **R** on McKenzie.
R on Willamette 1 block.
L on Pearl.
R on Harrison.

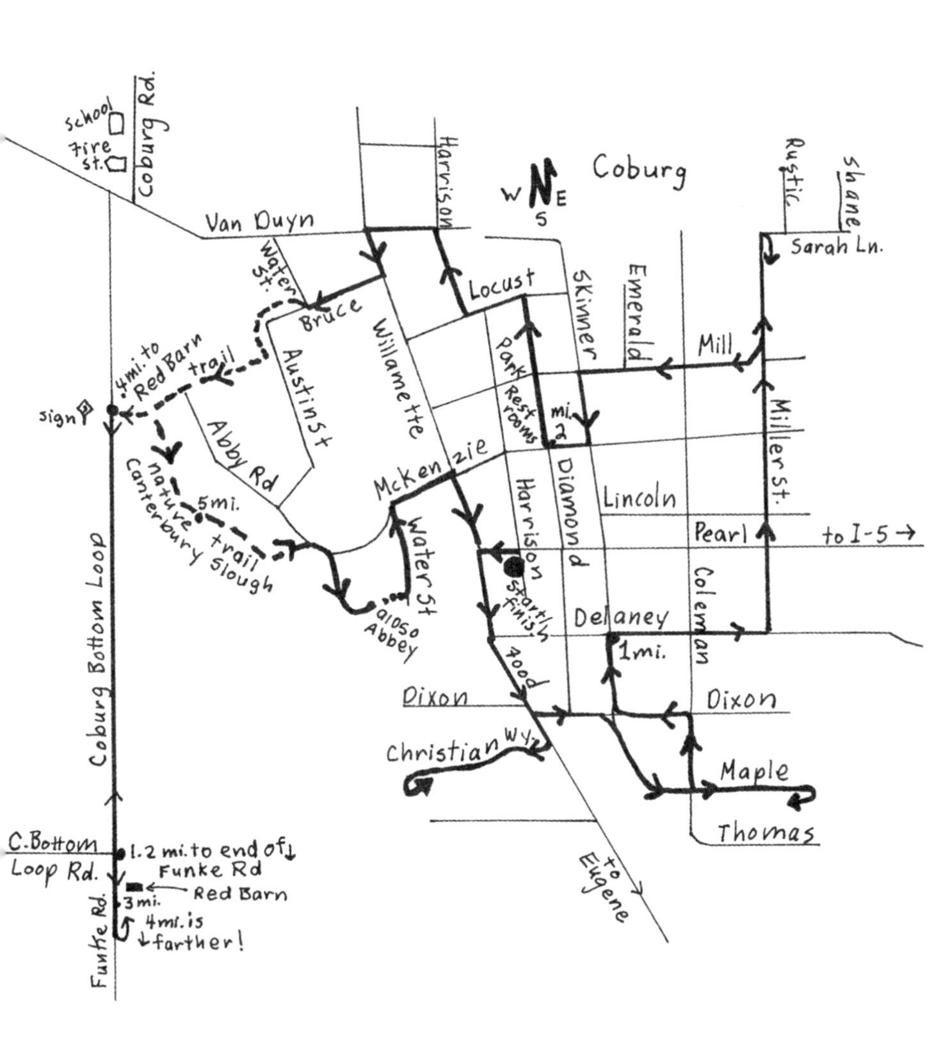
Coburg
W N E S
Coburg Rd.
school
Fire st.
Van Duyn
Harrison
Rustic
Shane
Sarah Ln.
Water St.
Bruce
Locust
Skinner
Emerald
Mill
Willamette
Austin St
Park
Rest rooms
mi. 2
4mi. to Red Barn
trail
sign
Abby Rd
Miller St.
Mckenzie
Harrison
Diamond
Lincoln
nature trail
Canterbury Slough
5mi.
Water St
Pearl
to I-5 →
start/finish
Coleman
Delaney
1mi.
91050 Abbey
4000
Dixon
Dixon
Christian Wy.
Maple
Thomas
to Eugene
Coburg Bottom Loop
C. Bottom Loop Rd.
1.2 mi. to end of Funke Rd
Red Barn
3mi.
4mi. is farther!
Funke Rd.

Corvallis Walks

page

1. Historic Downtown — 30
Includes Avery-Helm area
2 mile or 4 mile. Flat. Train depot.
Start at NW 1st and NW Tyler.

2. Franklin Park, Atomic Ranch — 32
Includes two historic areas.
2.2 mile or 3.8 mile. Flat.
Start at NW Tyler and NW 10th.

3. College Hill West — 34
Historic neighborhood.
2.5 mile, 27 ft. ascent.
Start at Harrison and 29th.

4. OSU Campus — 36
2.7 mile or 3.7 mile. Flat.
Start at SW 11th and Madison.

5. Willamette Park and Cemetery — 38
5 mile or 6.7 mile. Flat.
Start at SW 'B' St. and SW 2nd St.

6. Willamette Park — 38
2 mile or 3 mile. Flat.
Start at Willamette Park.

Historical information available at:
1.) www.visitcorvallis.com
2.) Visitor center at 553 Harrison.

Corvallis Start Points

For longer distance, connect the walks. See map.

- Walk #1 connects to #2 on Tyler, to #5 along river path, to #4 at 11th and Madison.
- Walk #2 connects to #1 on Tyler St. and to #4 at Madison and 11th
- Walk #3 connects to #4 at 26th.
- Walk #4 connects enroute to #1, to #2 at 11th to Tyler, #3 on 26th.
- Walk #5 connects to #1 on river path.
- Walk #6 expands into walk #5.

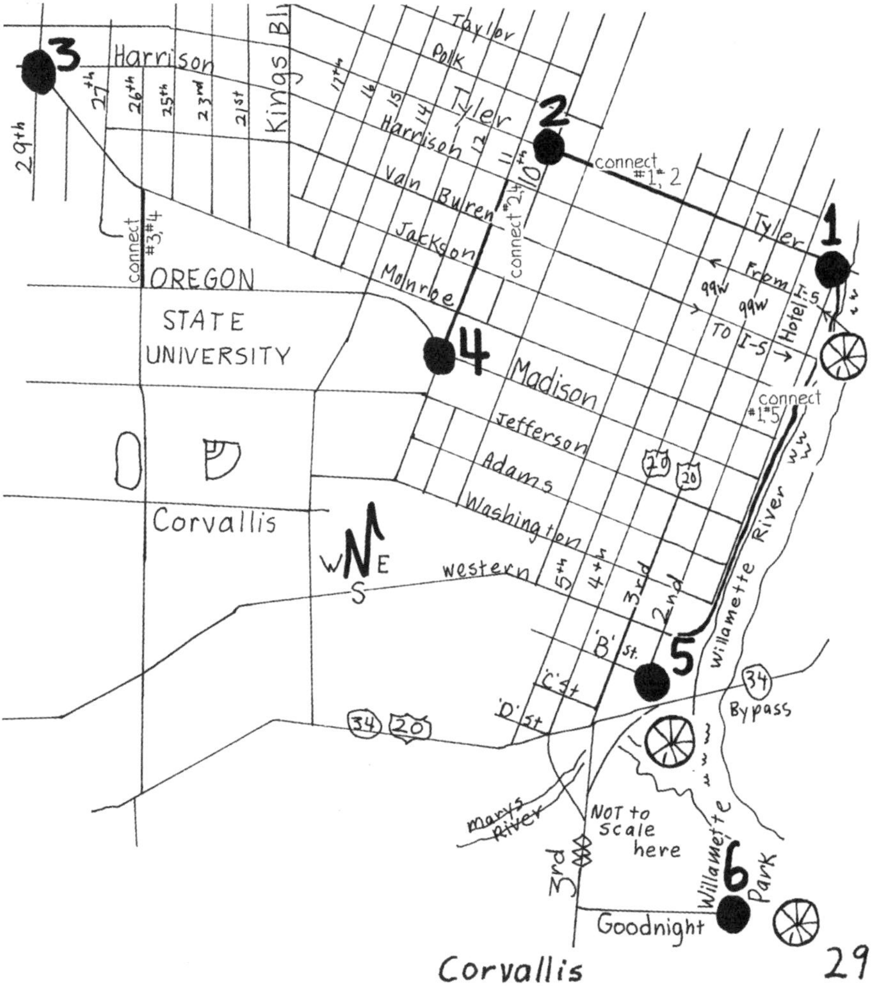

HISTORIC DOWNTOWN

Corvallis

Distance: 2mi. or 4mi. flat

Start/finish at NW 1st St. and NW Tyler, on Riverfront.

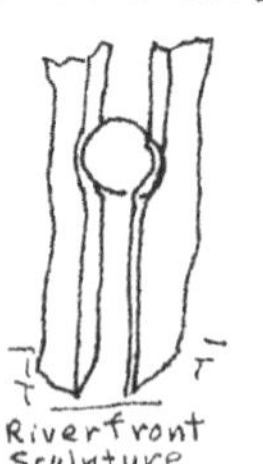
Riverfront Sculpture

From I-5, take exit 228.
R on NW 2nd, first street after bridge, for 1 block.
R on Tyler into free parking lot.
Restrooms in green building on path at Van Buren.

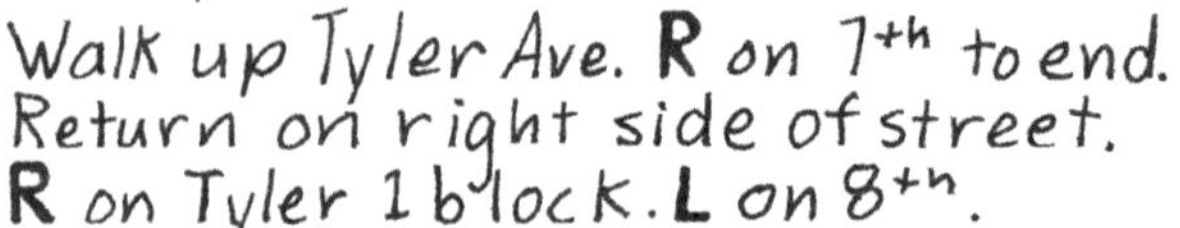

Walk up Tyler Ave. **R** on 7th to end.
Return on right side of street.
R on Tyler 1 block. **L** on 8th.

on 7th

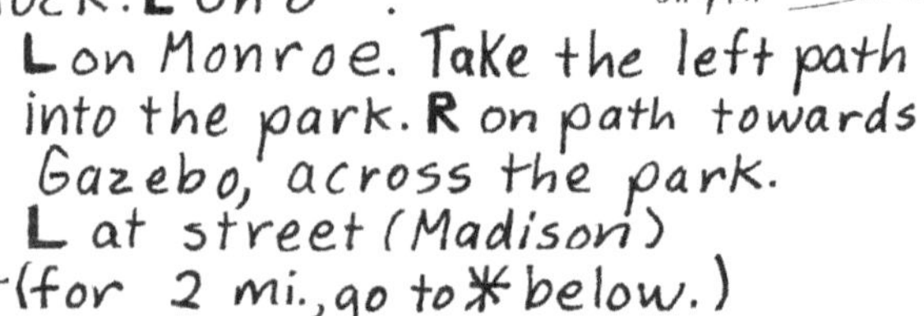

L on Monroe. Take the left path into the park. **R** on path towards Gazebo, across the park.
L at street (Madison)
(for 2 mi., go to * below.)

R on 5th to end. Return to B st.
L on B st, 1 block. **R** on 6th.
L on Washington. **R** on 8th.
L on Jefferson. **R** on 11th.

old Depot on washington

church door

R on Monroe.
* **L** on 4th to courthouse steps.
Return to 4th and Monroe.
Continue 1 block. Cross Madison, go **L**, 2 blocks.

R on SW 2nd St. 1 block.
L on Jefferson.
L on Riverfront path to finish.

at waterfront entry

History for Avery-Helm area available at www.visitcorvallis.com or Visitor Center, 553 Harrison.

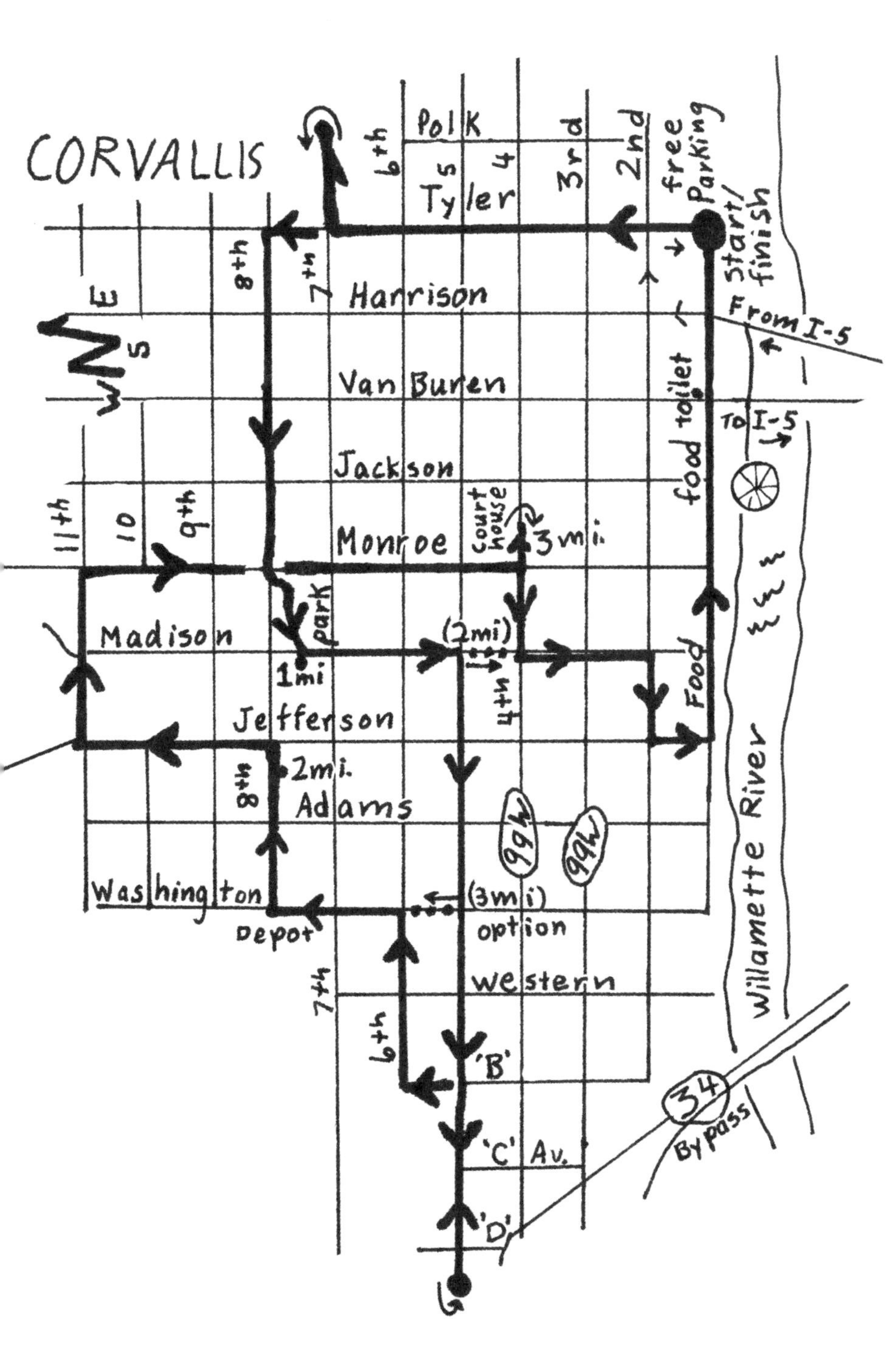
CORVALLIS
Polk
Tyler
Harrison
Van Buren
Jackson
Monroe
Madison
Jefferson
Adams
Washington
western
'B'
'C' Av.
'D'
2nd
3rd
4
5
6th
7th
8th
9th
10
11th
4th
free Parking
start/finish
From I-5
To I-5
food
toilet
Food
court house
3mi
(2mi)
1mi
park
2mi.
(3mi)
option
Depot
99W
99W
34
By pass
Willamette River

Franklin Park, Atomic Ranch

Corvallis

Distance: 2.2 mi. or 3.8 miles, flat.

Start/finish: NW Tyler Ave. and NW 10th St.
From I-5 take exit 228. **L** onto 34 OR.
Continue straight, on Harrison.
R on 10th. **L** on Tyler. Park on Street.

On Tyler, walk to 11th.
R on 11th. **L** on NW Filmore, 1 block.
L on 12th. **R** on Harrison, 1 block.
R on 13th. **L** on Filmore, 1 block.
L on 14th. **R** on Harrison, 1 block.
R on 15th. **L** on Taylor.

Tudor Style

(2.2 mi. option. **L** on 16th.
L on Van Buren. **L** on Tyler to end.)

To Atomic Ranch homes:
R on 16th. **R** on NW Beca, 1 block.
R on 15th. **L** on Lincoln.
L on 14th. **R** on Greely to end.
Return to 14th. **L** on 14th.

Atomic Ranch Style

R on Grant.
L on 17th.
L on Buchanan.
R on 16th.

L on Van Buren.
L on 11th, to Tyler. **R** on Tyler to end.

History brochure of neighborhood at
www.visitcorvallis.com or
Visitor Center, 553 Harrison.

1415 Lincoln "Ranch Redo"

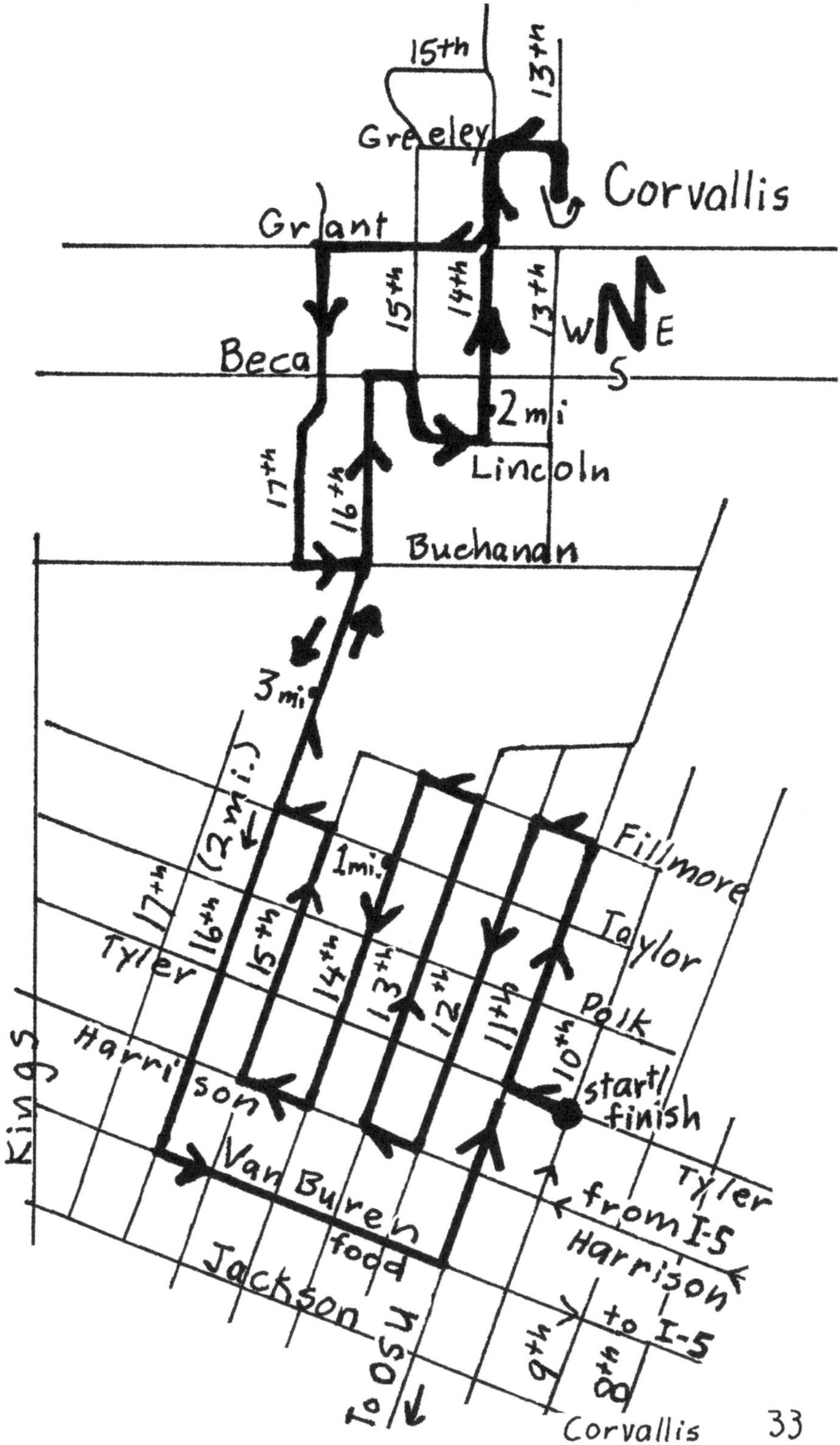

15th
13th
Greeley
Corvallis
Grant
15th
14th
13th
W N E
S
Beca
2 mi
Lincoln
17th
16th
Buchanan
3 mi
(2 mi.)
1 mi.
Fillmore
Taylor
17th
16th
15th
14th
13th
12th
11th
10th
Tyler
Polk
Kings
Harrison
start/
finish
Van Buren
food
Jackson
Tyler
from I-5
Harrison
to I-5
9th
8th
To OSU

COLLEGE HILL WEST

Corvallis

Distance: 2.5 mi. 27 ft. elevation gain
History brochures at www.visitcorvallis or Visitor Center, 553 Harrison, for neighborhood.

Start/finish: Harrison and 29th

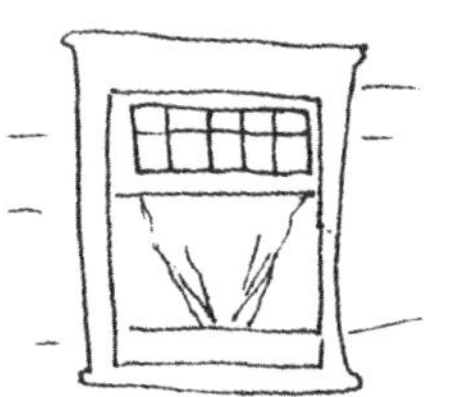

From I-5 take exit 228.
Continue straight, on Harrison.
R on 29th 1 block. **L** on Tyler.
Park on street. Walk back to Harrison and 29th.

Cross Harrison. Walk on right side of Arnold. R on 28th.
R at corner on Van Buren.

R on 35th. Cross Harrison, go **L.**
R on 36th. **R** on Polk 1 block.
R on 35th one block.

L on Tyler. **R** on 33rd one block.
L on Harrison one block.
R on 32nd.
L on Jackson one block.
R on 31st to end and return.

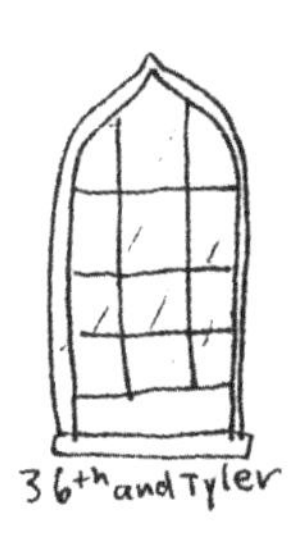

R on Harrison one block.
R on 30th one block.
L on Van Buren.
R on Arnold.
L on 25th.
L on Harrison to finish.

R on 29th. **L** on Tyler to your car.

Blueberries

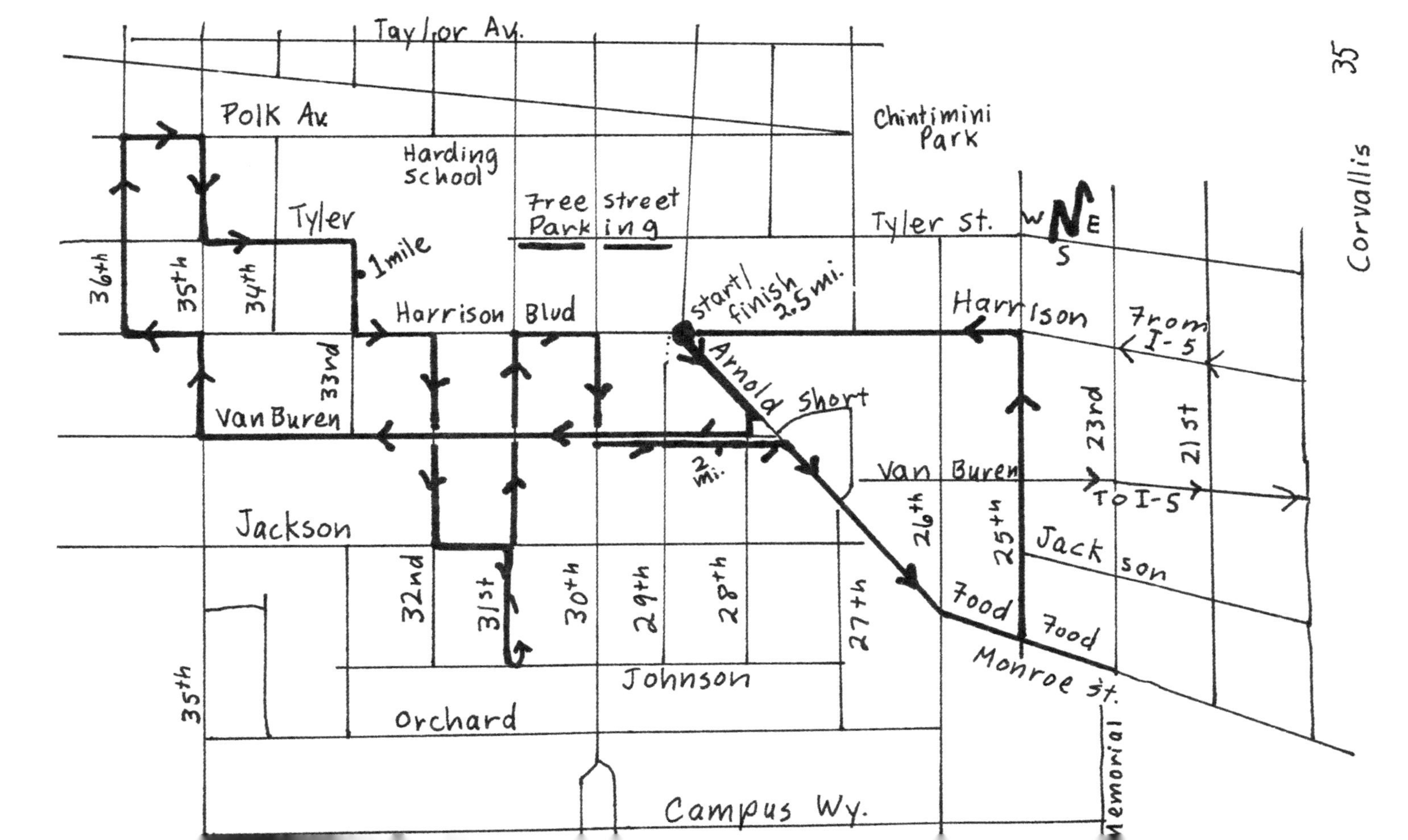
Taylor Av.
Polk Av
Chintimini Park
Harding School
Tyler
Free street Parking
Tyler St.
W N E S
1 mile
36th
35th
34th
Harrison Blvd
start/finish 2.5 mi.
Harrison
From I-5
33rd
Arnold
Short
Van Buren
23rd
21st
2 mi.
Van Buren
To I-5
Jackson
26th
25th
Jackson
32nd
31st
30th
29th
28th
27th
Food
Food
Monroe St.
35th
Johnson
Orchard
Campus Wy.
Memorial
Corvallis

Oregon State U. Campus

Corvallis

Distance 2.7 mi. or 3.7 mi. Flat.

OSU COW

Start/finish: SW 11th and SW Madison.

From I-5, take exit 228. Continue straight (on Harrison).
L on 11th to Madison.
Free street parking on 11th.

Enter campus on pedestrian path.
Stay on main sidewalk.
Cross street (14th). Take path to left, around building. Go straight on path. Pass Giant Sequioa grove on your left. At dead end, Cross street (SW 26th). Go **L**.
Cross next street (Jefferson).

Bent

Veer right, through Weatherford arch. Down steps on left.
R at street (Intramural).
R on 30th, 1 block.
L on Jefferson, 1 block.
R on SW 35th, 1 block.
(for 2.7 mi. **R** on Campus Way.)
see * below.)

weatherford Arch

Go to covered bridge, return, stay on Campus Way, through Campus.
***L** before Shepard Hall.
building, loop around rock in lovely garden, return to Campus Way.
L on Campus Way.

Irish Bend Covered Bridge

R on 15th.
L at crosswalk to sidewalk path.
Take middle path to finish.

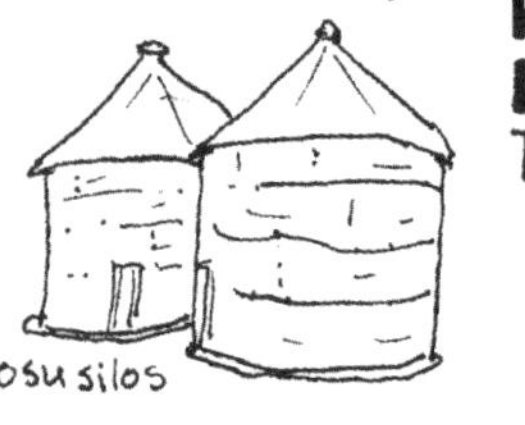
osu silos

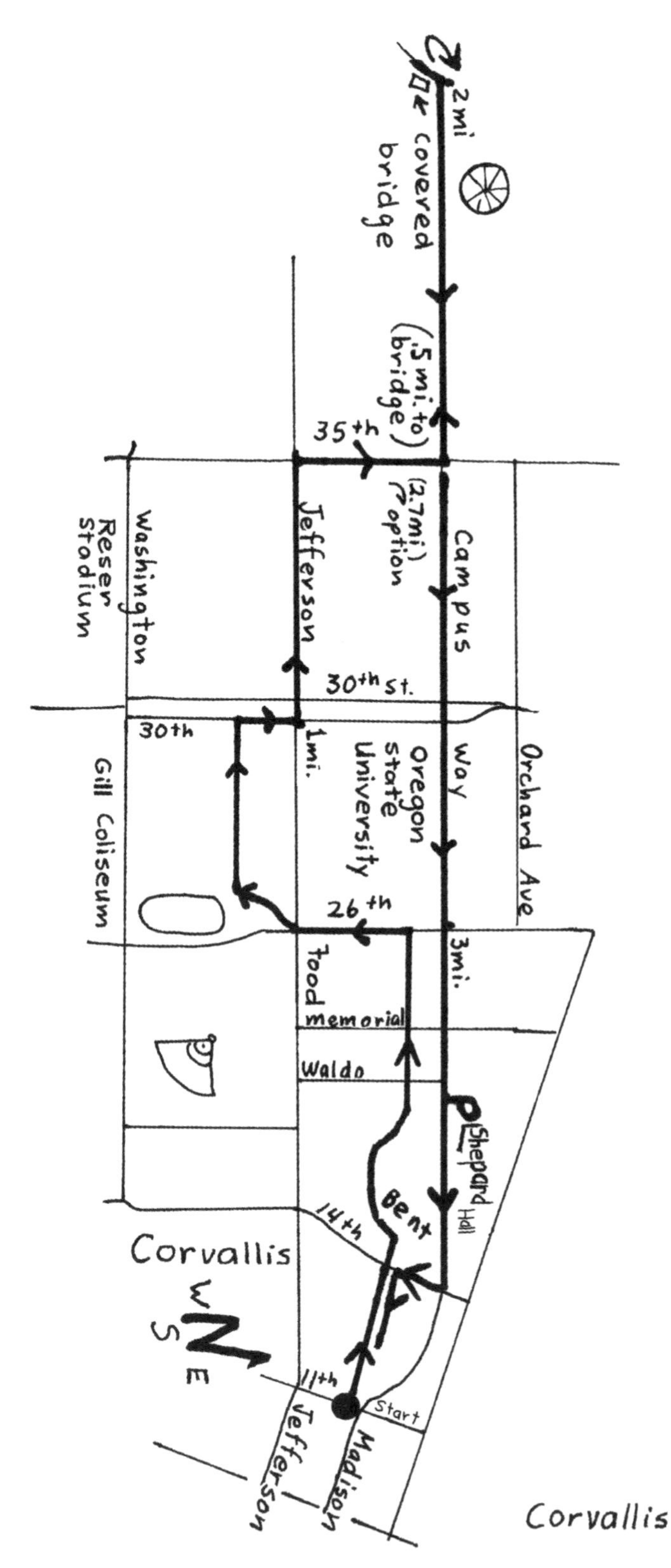

2mi
covered bridge
(.5mi. to bridge)
35th
(2.7mi) option
Jefferson
Campus Way
Washington
Reser stadium
30th st.
30th
1mi.
Oregon state University
Orchard Ave
Gill Coliseum
26th
Food memorial
3mi.
Waldo
Shepard Hall
Bent
14th
Corvallis
W
N
S
E
11th
Start
Jefferson
Madison

Willamette Park, Cemetery

Corvallis

Distance: 2 mi, 3 mi., or 5 or 6.7 miles. Flat.

- Start/finish for 2 mi. or 3 mile: Willamette Park.
  From I-5, exit 228. At 34 Bypass, go **L**.
  Take ramp to sw 4th, curve **R** on 3rd.
  L on Goodnight Ave. into Willamette Park.
- <u>for 2 miles</u>, walk back to Goodnight at Park.
  Follow from ■ below, back to park.
- <u>for 3 miles</u>, Walk to the river.
  L on river path, through athletic fields.
  L at parking lot. **L** on Crystal Lake, Park, Goodnight Ave, back to park.

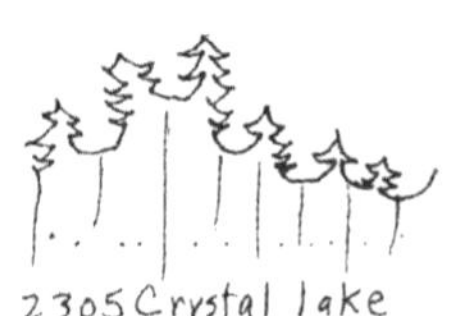
2305 Crystal lake

- <u>Start/finish for 5</u> and 6.7 miles: sw 'B' st. and sw 2nd.
  From I-5, exit 228. **L** on 34 Bypass.
  Ramp to 4th. Sharp **L** on 3rd.
  R on sw 'B' to parking lot.

Take path under highway. Stay **L** along river.
L on foot bridge over Marys River.
Cross Crystal Lk. Dr. go **L**.
At 1945 Crystal, cross street, enter cemetery.
Go straight, loop around this statue.
Return to Crystal, go **L**.

civil war veteran memorial

L on Park, curves left.
(for 5 mi, **L** on Goodnight to Park. follow at ◆ below to end.)
Cross Goodnight Ave.
■ Take path along treatment plant.
L at street (1250 Everglade)
At end of block, take path between houses. **L** at street (Shoreline).

2345 Crystal Lake

L on path after 3541 shoreline. ◆ **L** along river.
Go straight, pass Athletic fields. **L** at parking lot.
Cross street, Crystal, go **R**.
R on 3rd. Back across foot bridge.
L under highway bridge to finish.

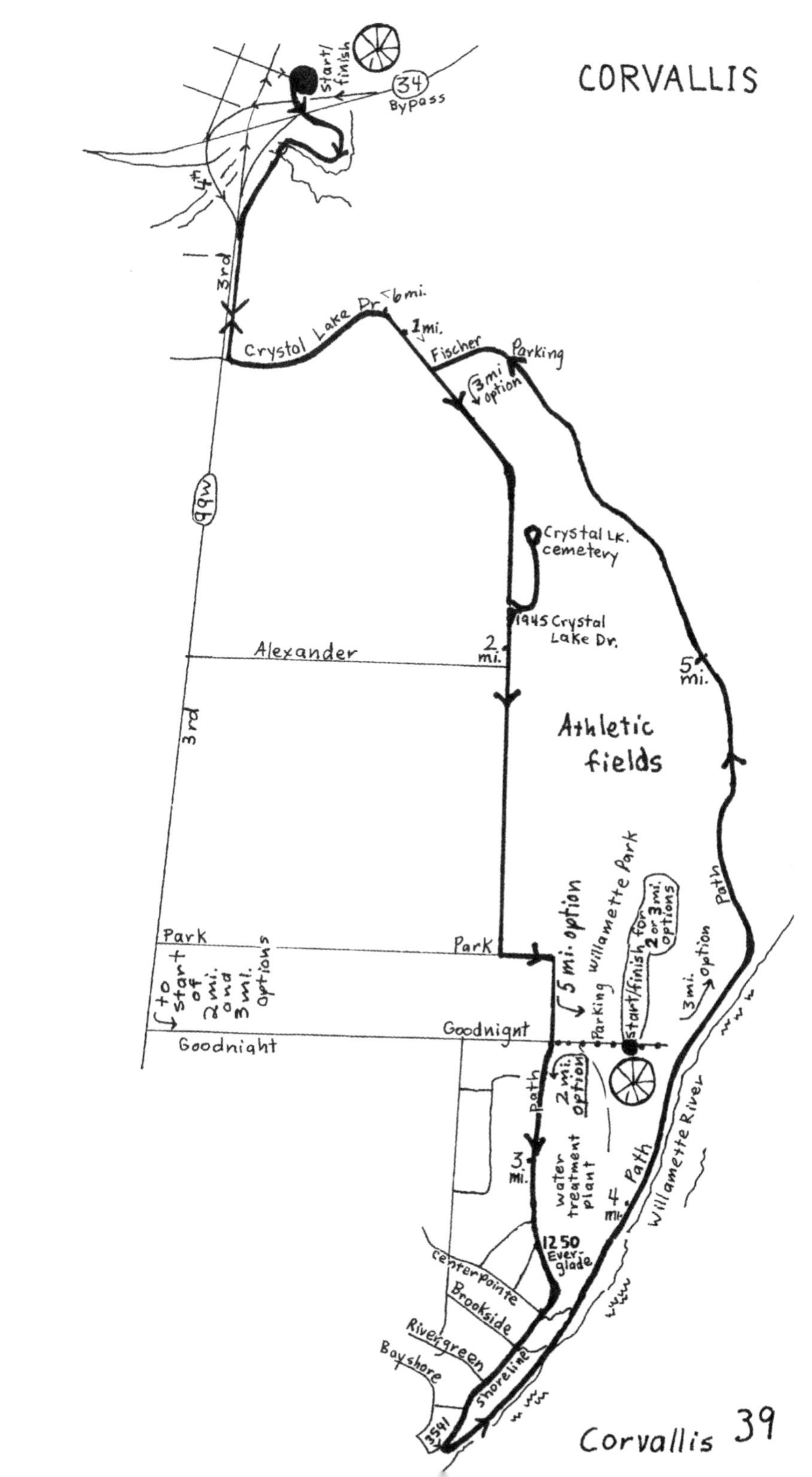

CORVALLIS
Start/finish
34
Bypass
4th
3rd
Crystal Lake Dr.
6 mi.
1 mi.
Fischer
Parking
3 mi option
99W
Crystal Lk. cemetery
1945 Crystal Lake Dr.
Alexander
2 mi.
5 mi.
Athletic fields
3rd
Willamette Park
start/finish for 2 or 3 mi. options
5 mi. option
Path
Park
Park
to start of 2 mi. and 3 mi. options
3 mi. option
Goodnight
Goodnight
Parking
2 mi. option
Path
3 mi.
water treatment plant
4 mi.
Path
Willamette River
1250 Everglade
Centerpointe
Brookside
Rivergreen
Bayshore
Shoreline
3541

HISTORIC COTTAGE GROVE

Distance: 2.8 mi. or 3.8 with extra loop. See •••

From I-5, exit at 174. follow signs to City Center.
R on Whitaker, 1 block, into free parking lot.
Start/finish: 8th and Gibbs.
L on Gibbs. The Visitor Center often has historical brochures.

439 So.1st Garden

L on 6th, 1 block. **R** on Whiteaker, straight on sidewalk along lot.
R across covered bridge.
Straight (on Main st.)

Cute house award

R on 'L' st. 1 block. **R** on Ash St.
L on River Rd, 1 block. **L** on Birch.
L on 'M' st. **L** on Old Mill Place into Silk Creek Park.
R on River Road.
After bridge, cross street, continue.

L on foot bridge over river.
R on So. 1st. **L** on Quincy, 1 block.
L on So. 2nd. **R** on Adams, 1 block.

1044 ash

L on 3rd. **R** on Washington, 1 block.
L on 5th, 1 block. **R** on Main, 1 block.
L on 8th to finish, or continue.

Stamp Mill

••• Add a mile: **L** on Gibbs.
R on Cherry.
R on Woods.
L on 7th. **R** on Grover.
L on 8th. **R** on Chadwick.
Cross 9th, go **L**
R on Thayer.
R on 10th, curves R into Gibbs.
Continue to finish at 8th.

147 'H' st 1897 church

window

39 'I' st.

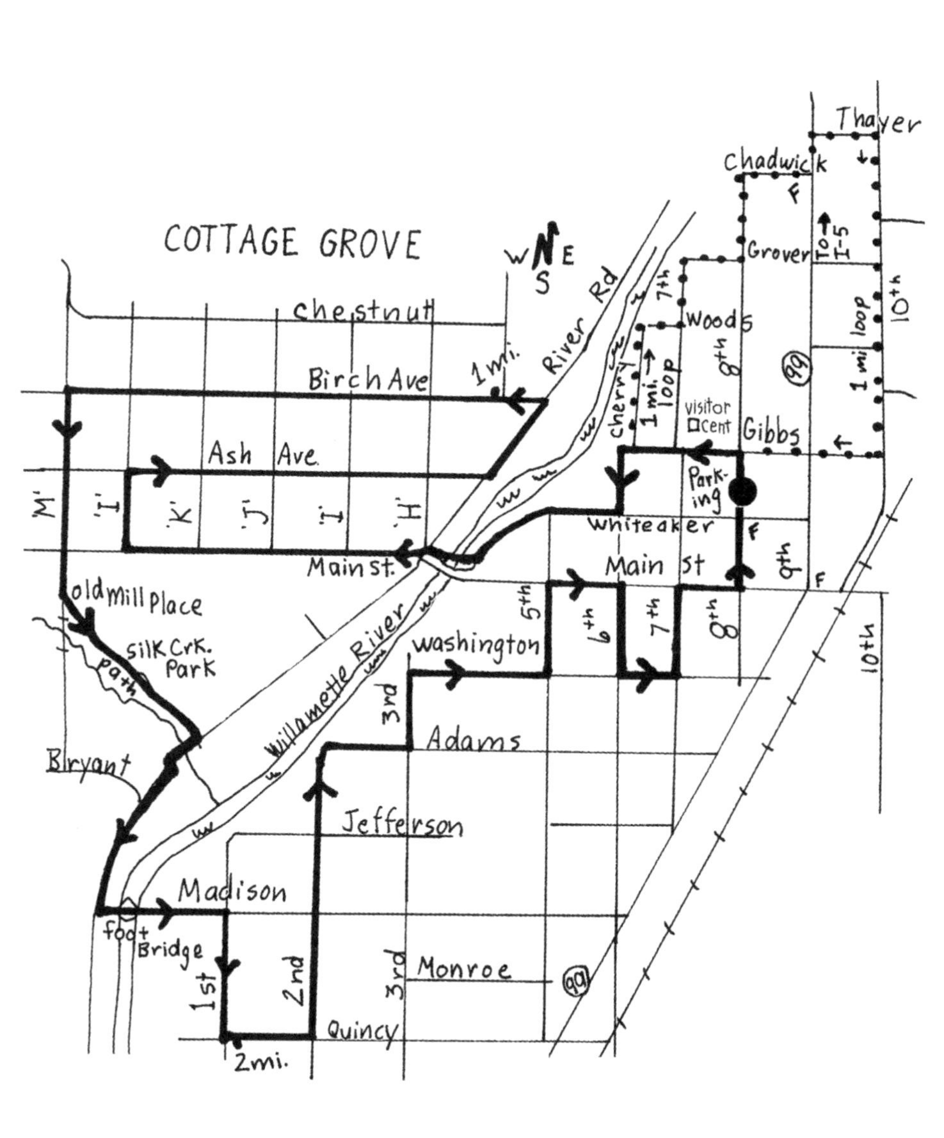
COTTAGE GROVE
W N E S
Chestnut
Birch Ave
1 mi.
River Rd
Ash Ave.
'M'
'L'
'K'
'J'
'I'
'H'
Main St.
Old Mill Place
Silk Crk. Park
path
Bryant
Willamette River
foot Bridge
Madison
1st
2nd
Quincy
2mi.
Jefferson
Adams
3rd
Washington
5th
6th
7th
8th
Main St
Monroe
99
Whiteaker
Park-ing
F
9th
10th
Gibbs
visitor cent
cherry
1 mi. loop
7th
Woods
8th
Grover
Chadwick
Thayer
To I-5
1 mi loop
10th

ROW RIVER TRAIL

Cottage Grove

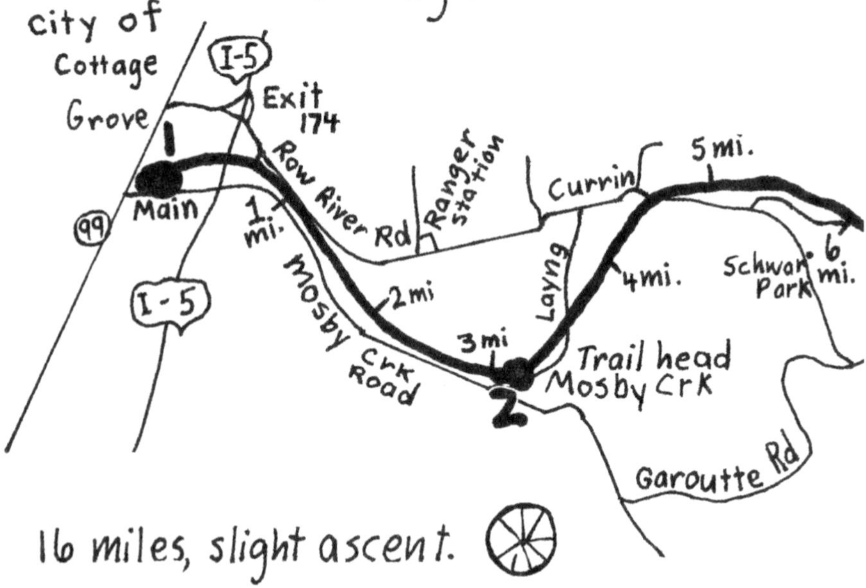

city of Cottage Grove
I-5
Exit 174
1
Main
99
1 mi.
Row River Rd
Ranger station
Currin
5 mi.
I-5
Mosby Crk Road
2 mi
3 mi
Layng
4 mi.
Schwarz Park
6 mi.
Trail head Mosby Crk
2
Garoutte Rd

16 miles, slight ascent.

Trail heads Directions from I-5.

1. Main St. and 10th St.
   Exit 174, follow signs to city center. **L** on Main St. **L** on 12th. Park behind Safeway.

2. Mosby Creek. Exit 174. Follow signs to Row River Rd. **R** on Row Rr. Con. 1 **R** on Row Rr. Con. 2. **L** on Mosby Cr.

3-7. Exit 174, follow signs to Row River Rd., to trailheads:
   3. Dorena Dam.
   4. Row Point (no restroom).
   5. Harms Park.
   6. Bake Stewart Park.
   7. Culp Creek.

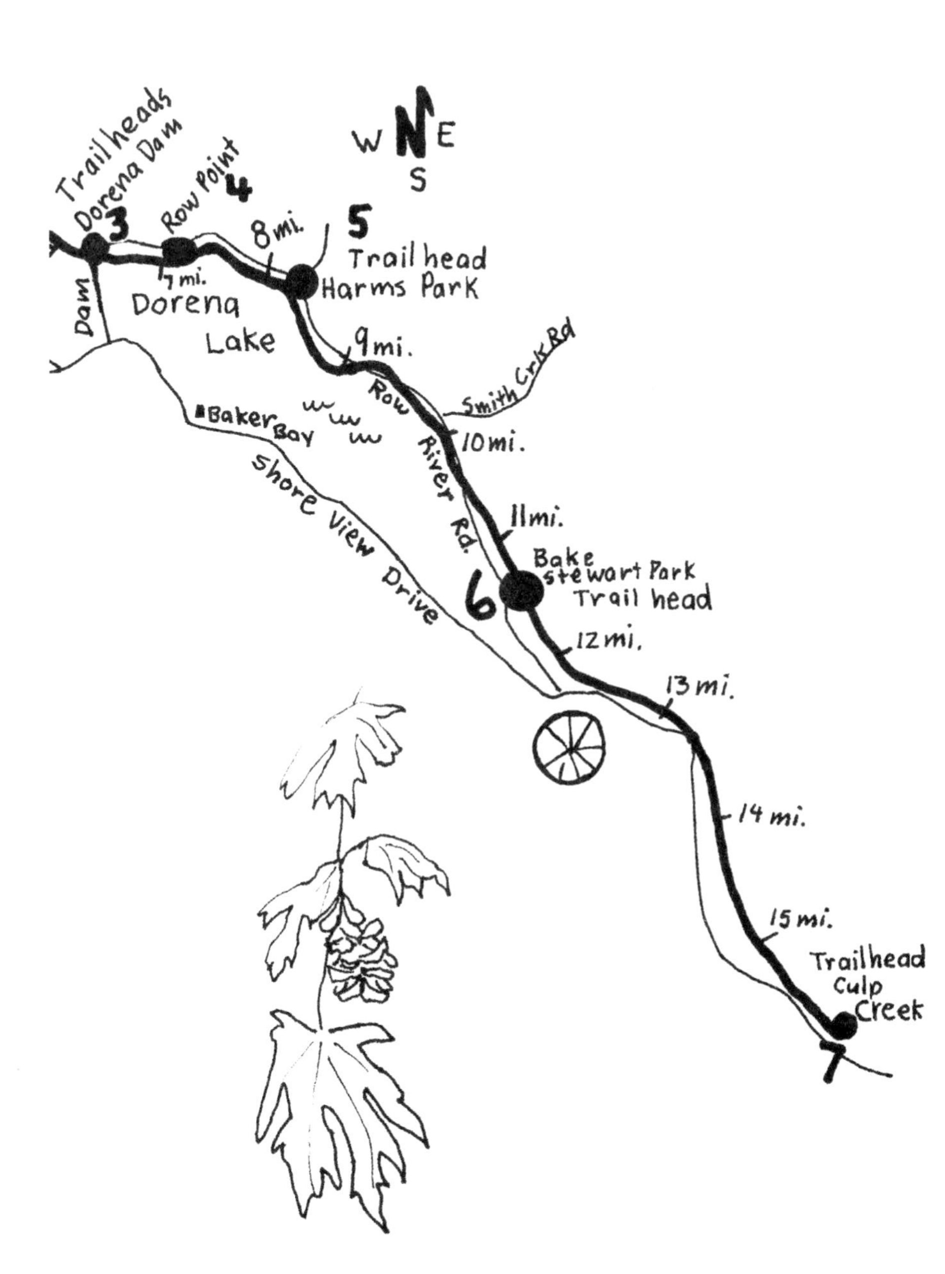

Trailheads
Dorena Dam
3
Row Point
4
W
N
E
S
5
Trail head
Harms Park
8 mi.
7 mi.
Dam
Dorena
Lake
9 mi.
Smith Crk Rd
Row
River
Rd.
Baker Bay
10 mi.
Shore View Drive
11 mi.
Bake
Stewart Park
Trail head
6
12 mi.
13 mi.
14 mi.
15 mi.
Trailhead
Culp
Creek
7

EUGENE

Directions from I-5 to alternate start point in free parking lot, past 155 High St.

From the north:
Exit 194B. Follow signs to downtown. Cross the bridge in the right lane. **R** on 3rd. **R** on High St. (no sign) to parking lot.

From the south:
Exit 192 to Eugene, on to Franklin Blvd. **R** at 5th St. Market (High St.)

Lodging near Amtrak:

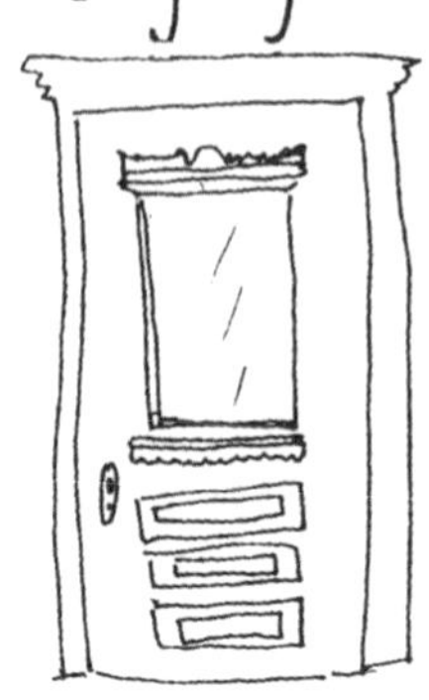

1. Hilton, Conference Center
   66 E. 6th 541-342-2000
2. Campbell Inn B+B, luxury
   252 Pearl, 541-343-1119
3. Downtown Motel, clean, okay
   301 W. 7th 1-866-221-6537
4. Courtesy Inn, clean, okay
   345 W. 6th 1-888-259-8481.
5. La Quinta Inn, pool, very nice.
   155 Day Island Rd. 541-344-8335

History: online at www.eugene-or.gov click on "Visitors" or the
- Eugene Visitor Center
  754 Olive St. M-Sa. 8-5 open

"Eugene, Oregon Walks", by Tyler Burgess
32 walking maps, is at the
Smith Family Bookstore
525 Willamette St. #9.97

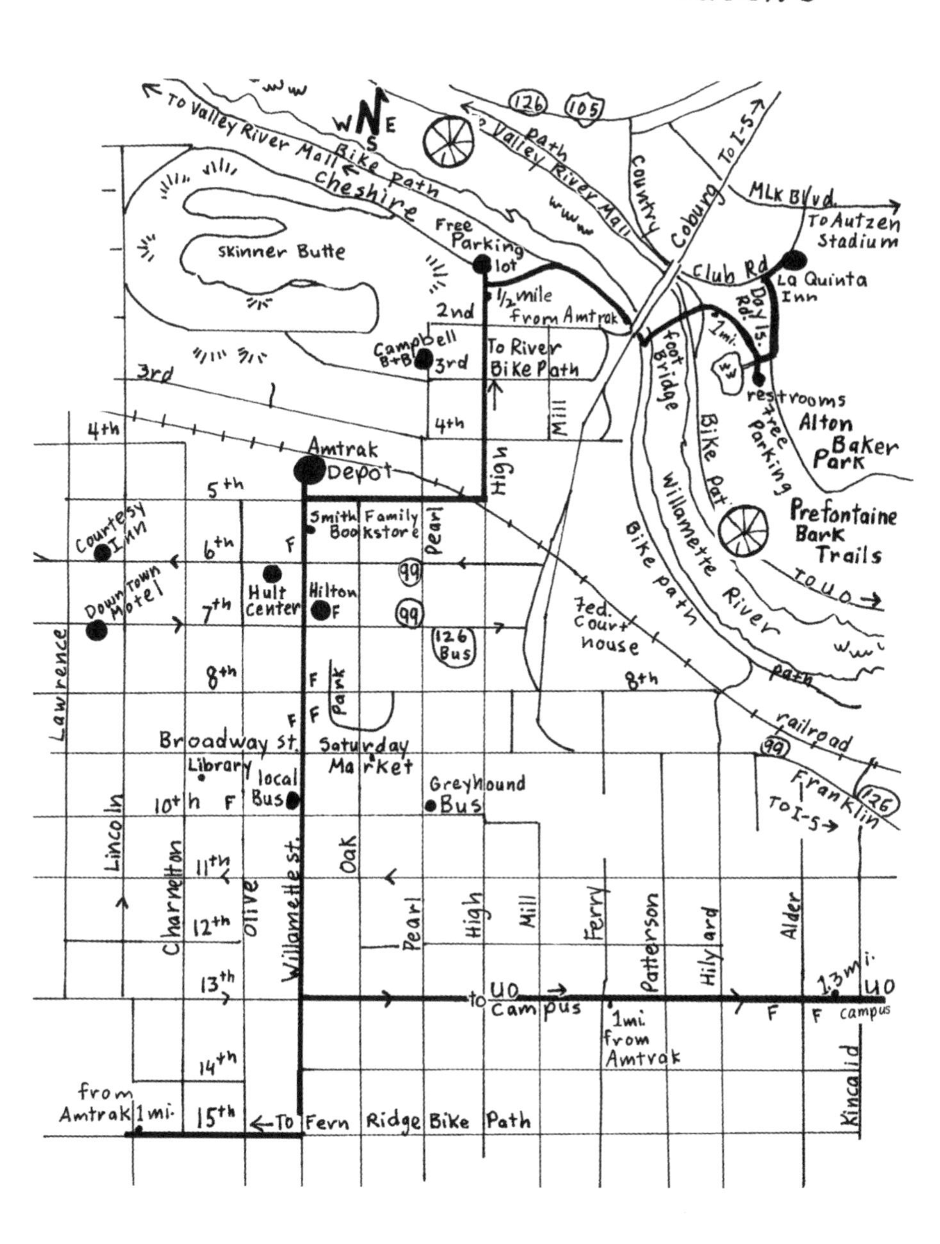
To Valley River Mall
Bike path
Cheshire
To Valley River Mall
Bike path
126
105
Country
Coburg
To I-5
MLK Blvd.
To Autzen Stadium
Skinner Butte
Free Parking lot
1/2 mile from Amtrak
Club Rd
La Quinta Inn
Day Is. Rd.
1 mi.
2nd
Campbell B+B
3rd
To River Bike Path
Mill
foot Bridge
restrooms
free parking
Alton Baker Park
3rd
4th
4th
Amtrak Depot
High
Bike Path
Willamette River
Prefontaine Bark Trails
To UO
5th
Courtesy Inn
6th
Smith Family Bookstore
Pearl
99
Downtown Motel
7th
Hult Center
Hilton
99
126 Bus
Fed. Court house
Bike path
Lawrence
8th
Park
8th
path
railroad
Broadway St.
Saturday Market
99
Library
local Bus
Greyhound Bus
Franklin
126
To I-5
10th
Lincoln
11th
Oak
Charnelton
12th
Olive
Willamette St.
Pearl
High
Mill
Ferry
Patterson
Hilyard
Alder
13th
to UO Campus
1mi. from Amtrak
1.3 mi.
UO campus
14th
Kincaid
from Amtrak 1 mi.
15th
To Fern Ridge Bike Path

TRAIN DEPOT to UO EUGENE

Distances: 2mi.* (no UO) or 3.7 mi. Flat.

Start/finish: Amtrak station, 433 Willamette.
or free parking past 155 High St.
Walk past parking lot to Willamette.
• At 525 Willamette, Smith Family Books, you can buy "Eugene Walks" $9.97.

L on Broadway. **R** on Pearl. **L** on 12th.

* for 2 mi., **L** on Patterson 1 block.
R on 11th. Cross Hilyard, go **L**.
Curves **L** on 8th. **On** rail tracks, go **L** to cross street. **R** on path.
Curves R, then **L** to 6th. **R** on High, by 5th St. Market. **L** on 5th to end.

R on Patterson, 1 block. **L** on 13th.
Cross Kincaid, go **L** to 12th.
R on sidewalk. **R** around Deady Hall.
R on first path. Cross street, go **L**.
R on path past Johnson Hall.

Cross street. Straight 50 paces.
R to Mother Statue. Continue up steps. Pass Hendricks Hall.
Go **L**. **L** at street, University, 1 block.

R on 13th **L** after Volcanology Dept.,
Cross Franklin Blvd., Go **L**.
Curves **R** on Hilyard.
Cross rail tracks, go to So. Bank trail. **L** on trail.

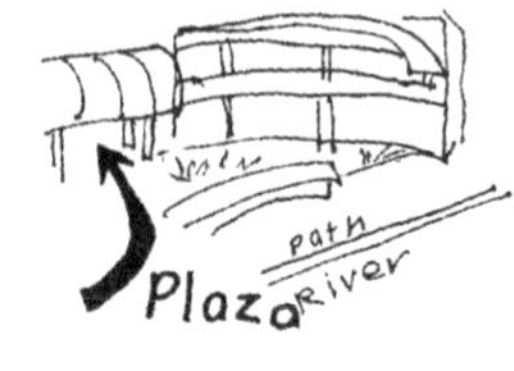

L in River Edge Plaza.
Straight to street (4th).
Cross the second street (High), go **L** 1 block.
R on 5th to end.

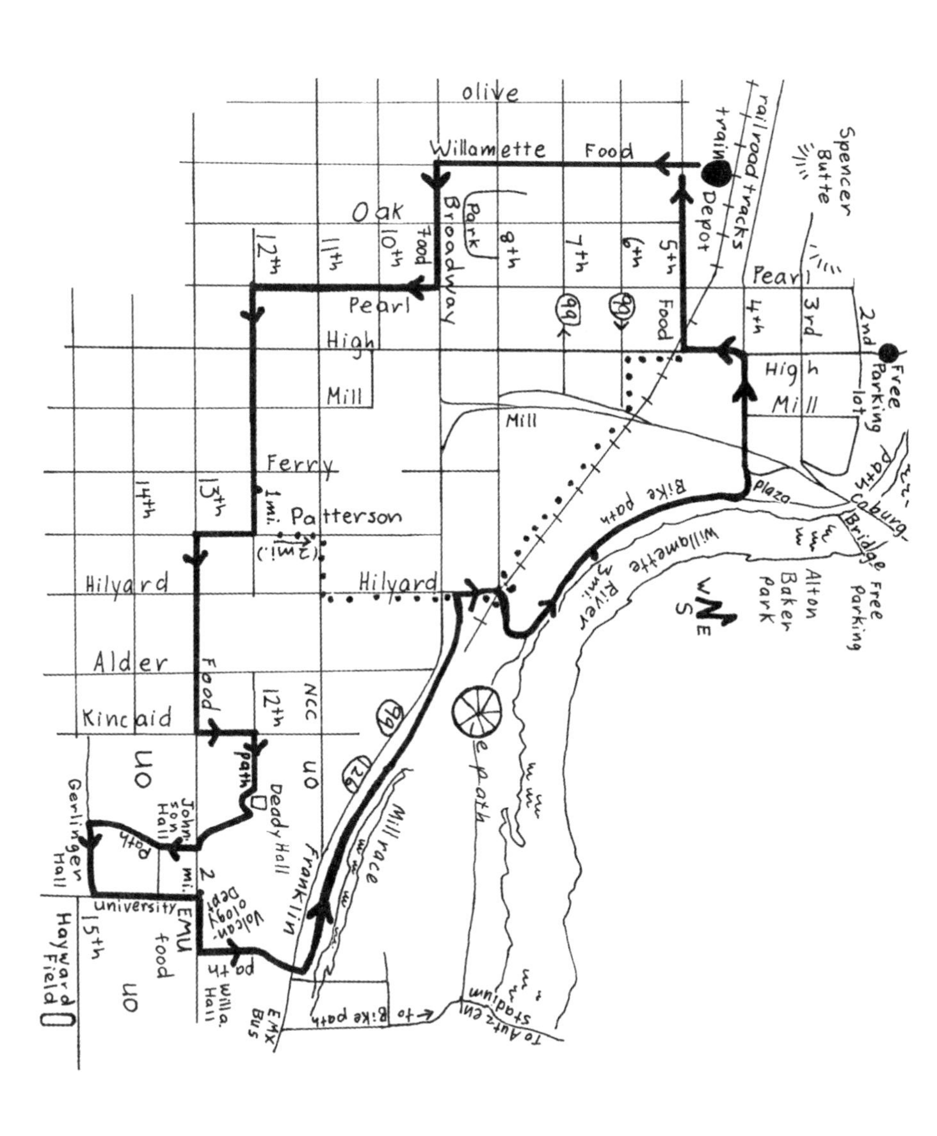
olive
Willamette
Food
train Depot
railroad tracks
Spencer Butte
Oak
Park
Broadway
Food
12th
11th
10th
8th
7th
6th
5th
Food
Pearl
Pearl
4th
3rd
2nd
High
High
Free Parking lot
Mill
Mill
Mill
Ferry
1 mi.
Patterson
(2 mi.)
14th
13th
Hilyard
Hilyard
Bike path
Plaza
Coburg
Bridge
path
Willamette River
3 mi.
Alton Baker Park
Free Parking
Alder
Food
Kincaid
12th
NCC
UO
UO
UO
path
Johnson Hall
Deady Hall
Gerlinger Hall
path
2 mi.
university
EMU
food
15th
Hayward Field
Volcanology Dept
Franklin
Millrace
path
Willa. Hall
EMX Bus
to Bike path
To Autzen stadium

SKINNER BUTTE

Distance: 2 miles, 124 feet ascent

Start/finish: Amtrak station, 433 Willamette St.
Or enroute at free parking lot,
past 155 High St.

From train, walk through parking lot to 5th Ave. and Willamette St.
L on 5th Ave. **L** at end. (High St.)
Curve **L** at parking lot.
At end of parking lot, at the second sign, cross street. Go **R.** Up steps to trail.

Follow any path going up.
On top of butte, continue **R.**
Pass flagpole, continue to picnic table, water fountain.

Return to flagpole. Walk past 30 paces. Go downhill on the path to your Left. It is steep, with steps.

Cross the road.
L for 30 paces.
R down path.
L to big Victorian, green house. Walk around to view front. Exit on driveway.

Shelton-M-Johnson
House Tours $5
T-F 10-1 S.S. 1-4
541-484-0808

R at street, Pearl.
R on 5th Ave.
R on Willamette St. to train.

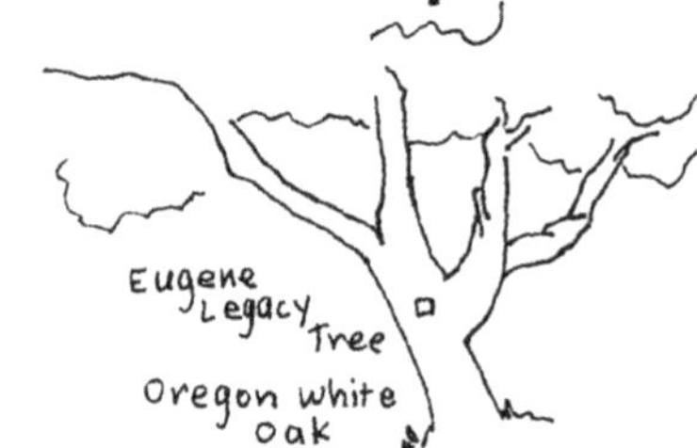

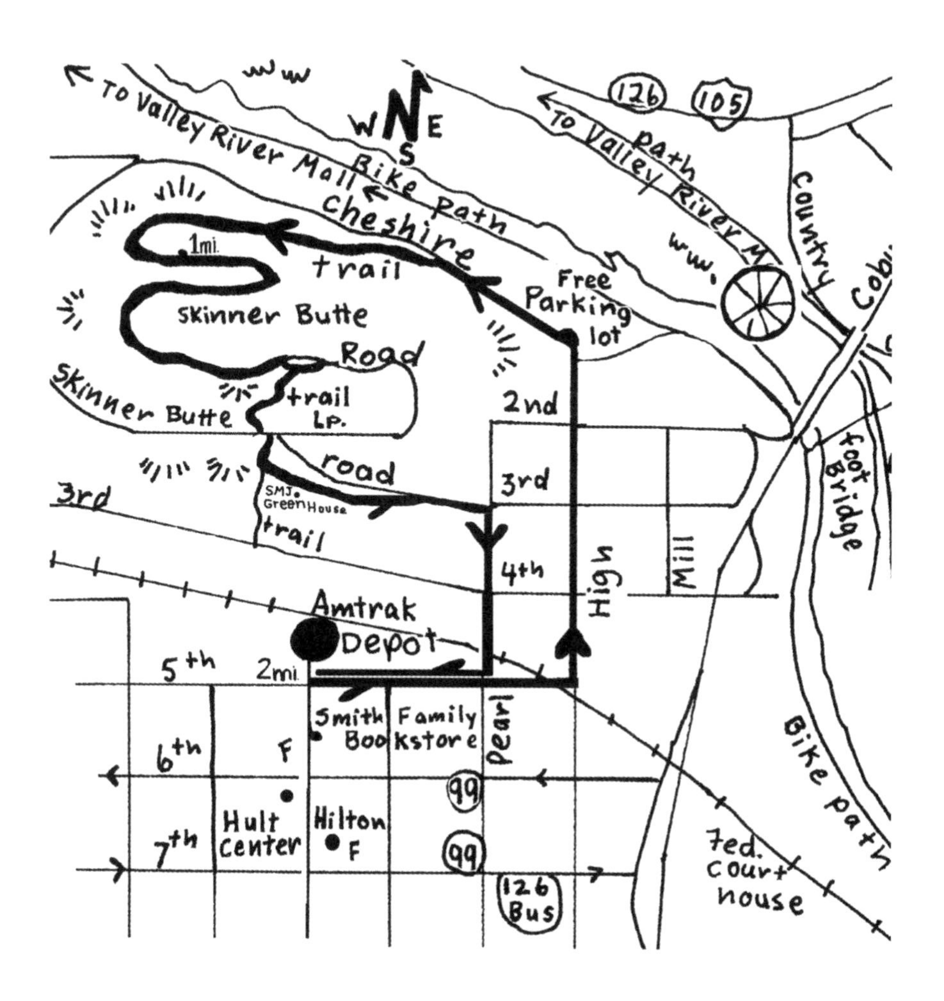
To Valley River Mall Bike Path
W N E S
To Valley River path
126
105
Cheshire
trail
1mi.
Skinner Butte
Road
Free Parking lot
Country
Skinner Butte
trail LP.
2nd
road
3rd
SMJ Green House
3rd
trail
foot bridge
4th
Mill
High
Amtrak Depot
5th
2mi.
Smith Family Bookstore
Pearl
6th
F
99
Hult Center
Hilton
F
7th
99
126 Bus
Fed. court house
Bike path

EUGENE RIVER BIKE PATH

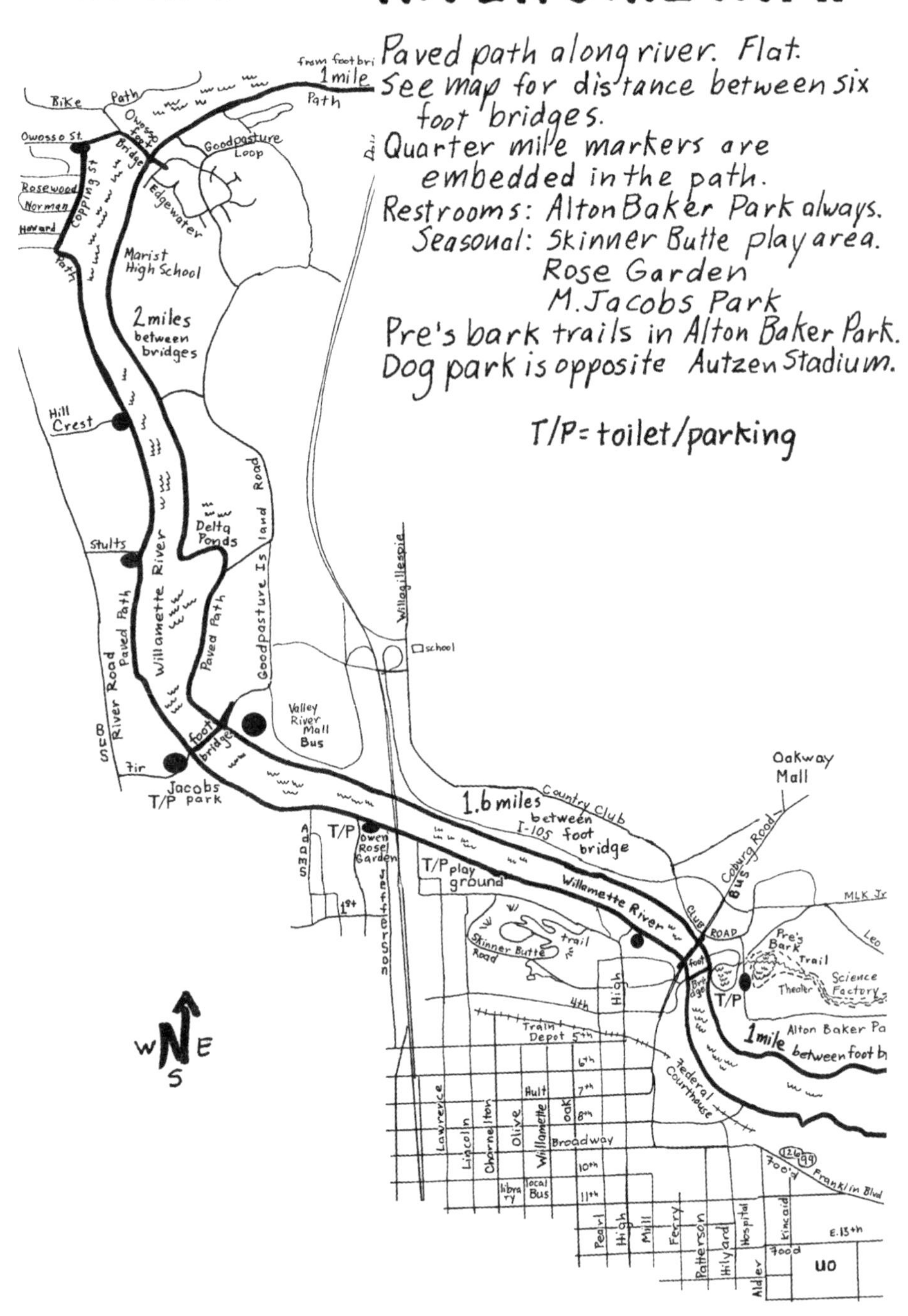

BIKE PATH ETIQUETTE

Walk or ride on right side.
Keep 2 abreast to let people pass.
Announce your presence when passing. "On your left."
Dogs must be leashed. It's the law.
Scoop dog poop.
Use a light when dark.
Nod, smile, say hello to everyone.

Bus: Valley River Mall. Bike path is behind mall, along river.

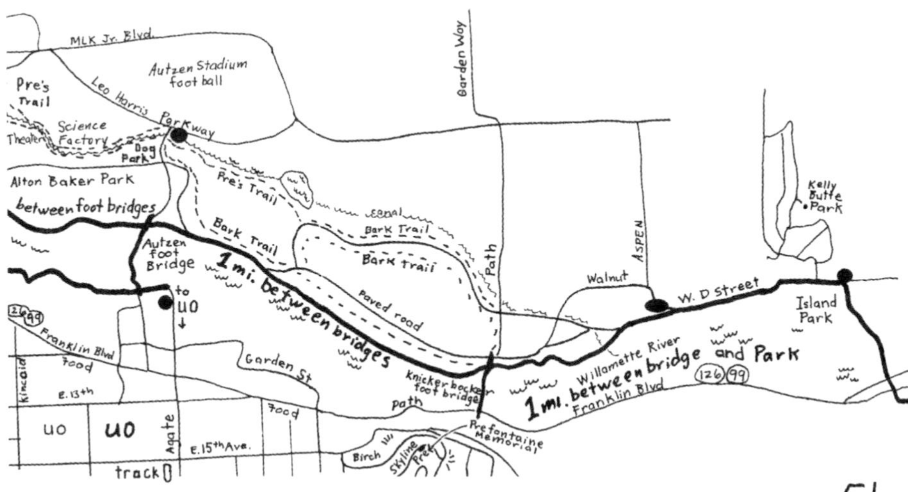

GOLD HILL

Distance: *1 mi., •1.6 mi., 3.4 mi. or 5 mi. Flat

From I-5, exit 40. Follow signs to Gold Hill. **R** on Dardanelles, for one block, into parking lot. No public restroom.

Follow paved path along 4th, going towards bridges over river. **L** at fork. *(or right for 1 mi. see * below.) Just before tennis courts, **R** on trail. Cross boat launch. Rejoin paved path. Turn around at end by power house, taking paved path back. Go straight under bridge.

cute house award

at Riverside and Dardanelles

*
R up path in park.
L on Chavner.
R on Riverside, 2 blocks.
R on Estremando, to rose-color house (no sign), museum.
L on 1st
R on Fredenburg. **R** on 2nd.
L on Dardanelles to end the 3.4 mile and 1 mile options.

Jail behind Museum
504 First
open 12-4
Thurs. - Sat
541-855-1182

on Second at Estramode

For 5 mile option, or •1.6 mile, continue up Dardanelles.
L on 5th.
L on Kellogg.
L on 4th.
R on Gustaf to 2nd to view old farm house, return to 4th.
R on 4th to finish.

Gustaf and Second

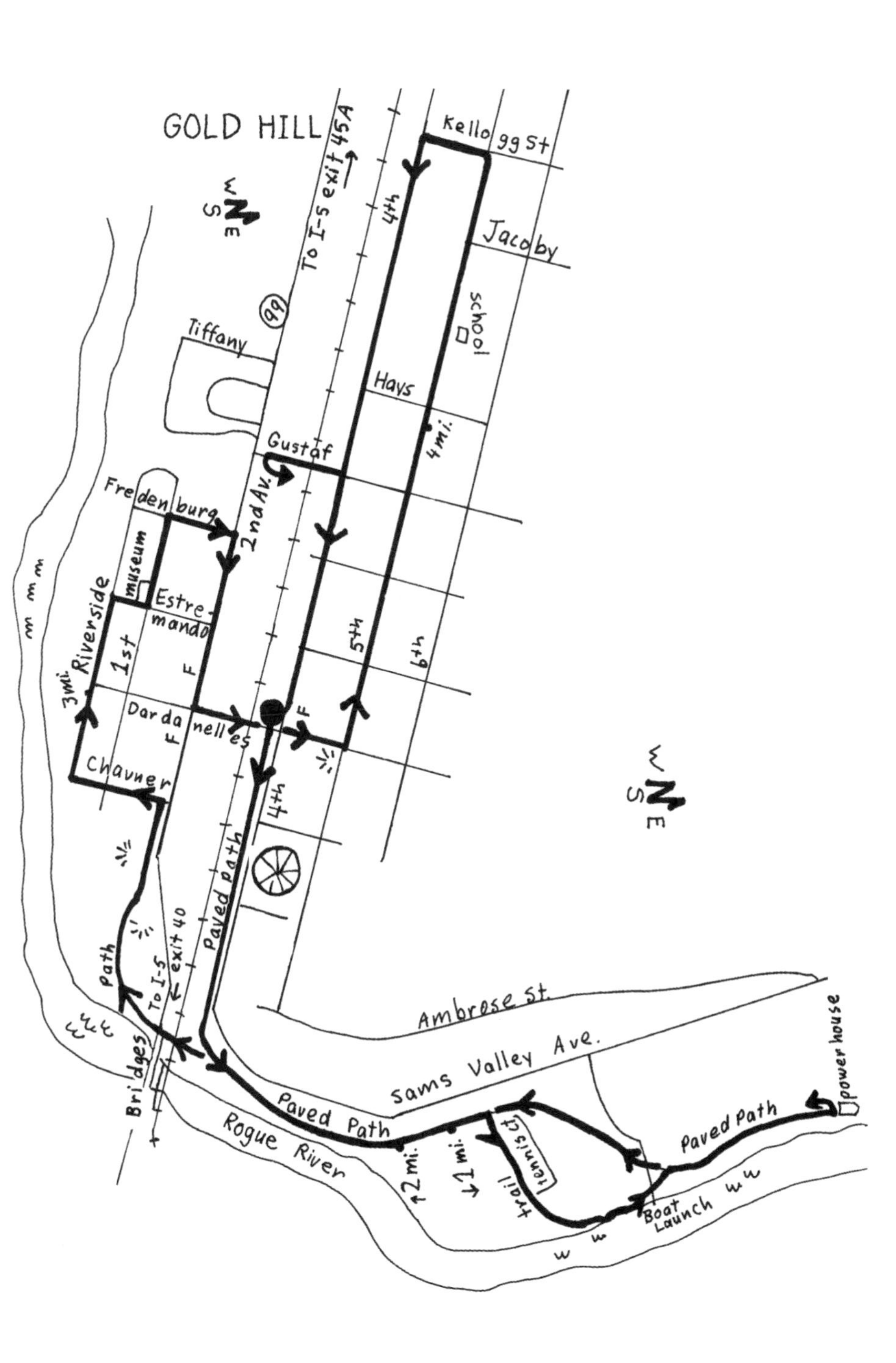
GOLD HILL
Kellogg St
Jacoby
To I-5 exit 45A
4th
99
school
Tiffany
Hays
4mi.
Gustaf
2nd Av.
Fredenburg
museum
Estremando
Riverside
1st
F
3mi.
Dardanelles
F
5th
6th
Chavner
4th
Paved Path
To I-5 exit 40
Path
Bridges
Ambrose St.
Sams Valley Ave.
Paved Path
Rogue River
2mi.
1mi.
trail
tennis ct
Boat Launch
Paved Path
power house

DOWNTOWN to MIDLAND

Grants Pass

Distances: ▲1 mi. * 2 mi., ° 2.8 mi. or 3.6 mi. Flat.

From I-5 north: Exit 58 to Redwoods, to Grants Pass.
From I-5 south: Exit 55 to Redwoods, to Grants Pass.

R on 'G' st. Free parking all day, between 3rd and 4th st.
On 'G', walk back to 6th.

R on 6th. **R** on 'I' st. **R** on Pine. ▲(for 1 mi, **R** on 'G'.)

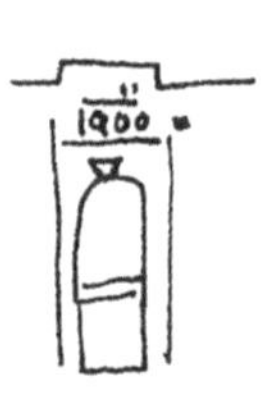

R on 'G' 1 block. **L** at fork.
L at Debo Park. Use crosswalk.
R for 1 block.
L across 'F' st.
Straight on to 3rd st. which becomes Lawnbridge.
*(**R** on 'A' for 2 mi. **R** on 6th, **R** on G)

L on Manzanita, 1 block.
R on Hawthorne.
R on Midland, 1 block.
R on Lawnridge.

°(for 2.8 mi. **R** on Manzin.) see ° below.

L on Manzanita, 1 block.
R on Washington, 1 block. °
L on Evelyn, 1 block.
R on Conklin.

L on 'A' st. 1 block.
R on 6th st.
R on 'G' to end.

5th and SW G

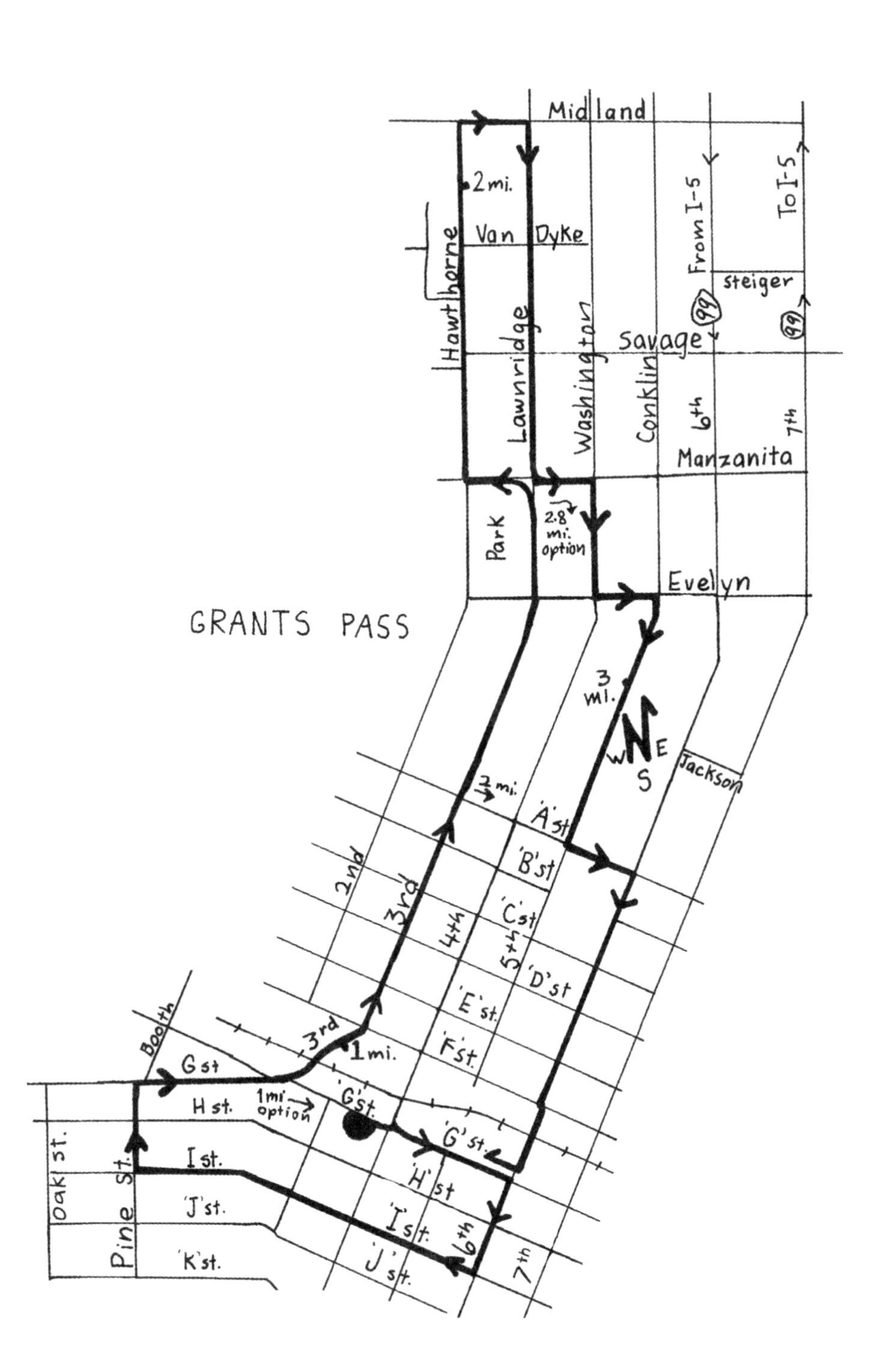
Midland
2mi.
Van Dyke
Hawthorne
Lawnridge
Washington
Conklin
From I-5
To I-5
steiger
99
Savage
6th
7th
Manzanita
Park
2.8 mi. option
Evelyn
GRANTS PASS
3 mi.
N
W
E
S
Jackson
1 mi.
'A'st
'B'st
'C'st
'D'st
'E'st.
'F'st.
2nd
3rd
4th
5th
Booth
G st
3rd
1mi.
H st.
1mi option
'G'st.
'G'st.
'H'st
I st.
'I'st.
'J'st.
'J'st.
'K'st.
Oak St.
Pine St.
6th
7th

DOWNTOWN to RIVER

Grants Pass

Distances: ▲1 mi., *2 mi., °3.6 mi, 5 mi. Flat.

From I-5 north: Exit 58 to Redwoods, to Grants Pass.
From I-5 south: Exit 55 to Redwoods, to Grants Pass.
R on 'G' st. Free parking all day between 3rd and 4th.
On 'G', walk back to 6th.

R on 6th. Cross bridge. ▲(for 1mi. **R** on 'M', **R** on 4th to end.)
Down steps at end.
R under bridge. Walk along river.
Circle playground. (restrooms).
Return across bridge *(for 2mi. **L** at 'M', **R** on 4th to end.)

L at 'M' st. 1 block. Cross 5th, go **L**.
R on Central, curves into Ballinger.
L on Greenwood into river path. ← (° for 3.6 mi. **R** on Greenwood see ● below.)
L at 'T' in path. **R** at fork in path. ●
Up and over bridge. Enjoy view.
Return. At end of bridge,
L down steps.

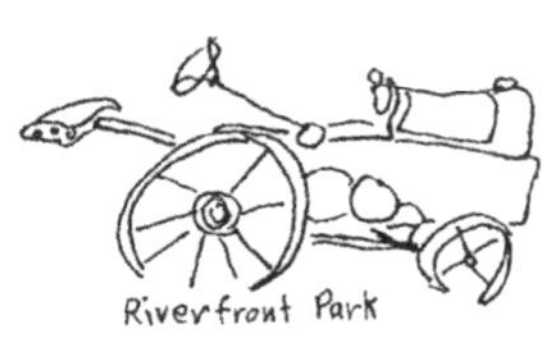

Riverfront Park

612 SW 4th

Straight across parking lot to trail.
R at fork. Over arch bridge, to play grounds. With your back to the restrooms,
L along parking lot.
Pass Sports Complex.

6th and M st.

Emerge on Webster.
L on Cottonwood, for 1 block.
R on Brownell.
L on Greenwood. **R** on Rogue River, 1 block.
L on Laurel. **R** on 'L' st.
L on Pine. **R** on 'G' st. to end.

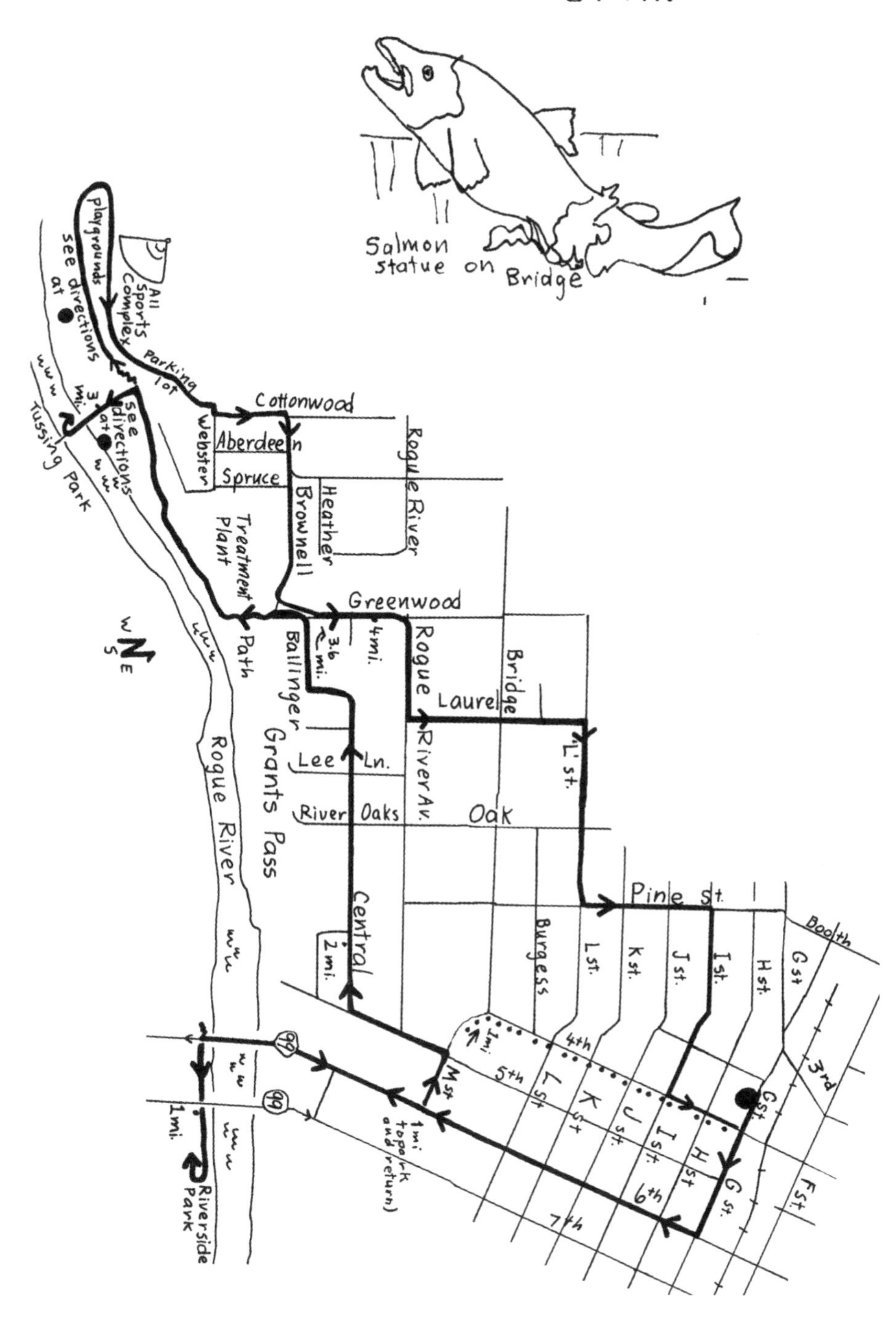
Salmon statue on Bridge
Playgrounds
see directions at
All Sports Complex
Parking lot
Cottonwood
Webster
Aberdeen
Spruce
Brownell
Heather
Rogue River
Tussing Park
see directions at
Treatment Plant
Path
Greenwood
Ballinger
3.6 mi.
4 mi.
Rogue River Av.
Bridge
Laurel
'L' st.
Lee Ln.
River Oaks
Oak
Grants Pass
Rogue River
Pine st.
Central
2 mi.
Burgess
L st.
K st.
J st.
I st.
H st.
G st
Booth
3rd
4th
5th
M st
6th
7th
F st.
1 mi
1 mi to park and return)
99
1 mi.
Riverside Park

JACKSONVILLE

Directions from I-5.

From the north, Exit 33 toward Central Point.
R on Pine, on to Hanley Rd.
From the south, Exit 30 toward Medford, Hwy 238.
L on 62, Crater Lake HWY, to Rossanley Dr.
L on Hanley Rd.

DOWNTOWN JACKSONVILLE

hand hewn fence posts

Distance: 1.3 mile. Flat.

Start/finish: Parking lot behind library.
(Restrooms in Junction Building.)

Walk back to entrance, up steps on right, toward Britt Gardens.

Cross street (California), go **L**.
Cross next street (Main), go **R** for 1 block.
L on Oregon St.

Long Tom for gold mining

Cross 'E', go **R** 1 block. **R** on 3rd.
L on Main, 1 block. **L** on 4th.
R on 'E', 1 block. **R** on 5th.
R on California.
Just before the library, **R** on path along the fence, to end.

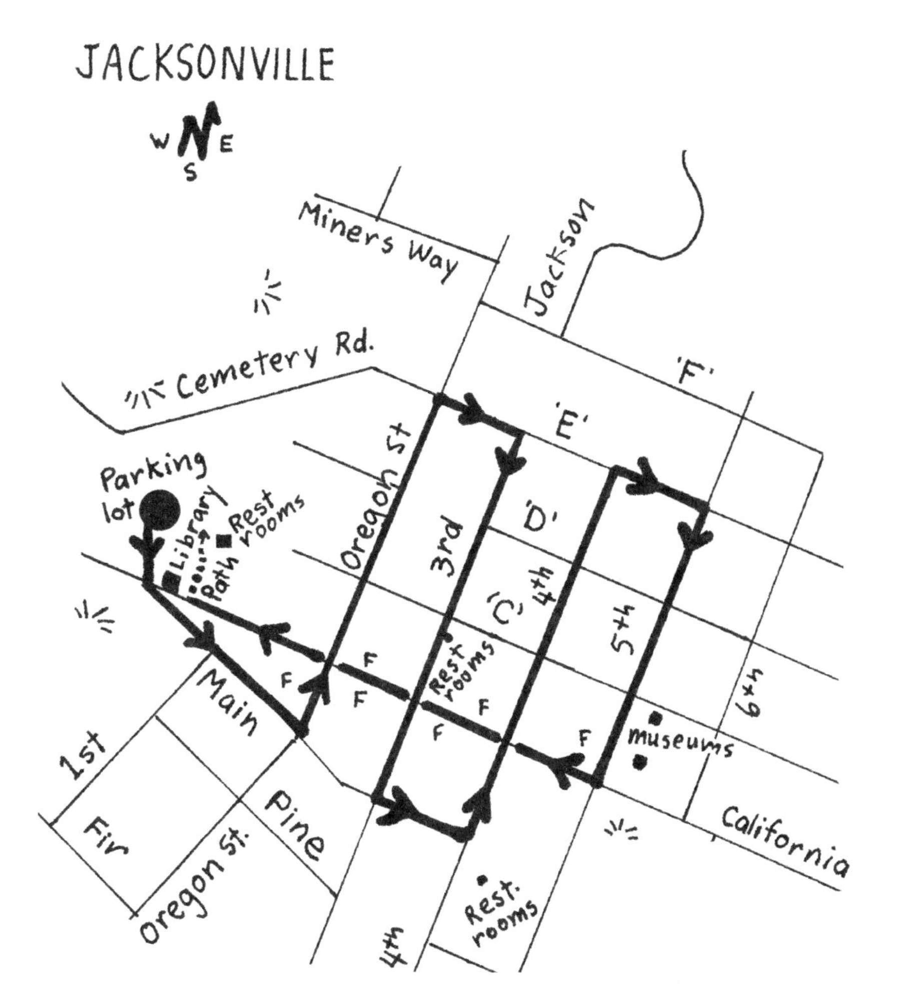
JACKSONVILLE
W N E
S
Miners Way
Jackson
Cemetery Rd.
'F'
'E'
'D'
'C'
Parking lot
Library
Path
Rest rooms
Oregon St
3rd
4th
5th
6th
Rest rooms
F
museums
Main
1st
Fir
Oregon St.
Pine
California
4th
Rest. rooms

AROUND DOWNTOWN

Jacksonville

Distance: 4 miles, slight hill

Start / finish: Parking lot behind library, off California Street.

Go to the far right corner of the parking lot.
Up the road to the cemetery.
Straight to tool house.

L on path to end, go **R** and **R** again on paths, pass tool house, go straight to restrooms, return to tool house, back down hill on road.

L on Oregon. **R** on Nunan.
Through Nunan Sq. **R** at end
R on Jackson Alley. **L** at Street.
After house no. 200, before no. 170.
L on round stone path.
R on boardwalk. **L** at each fork.
L at the street, ("F").

Cross 5th St., go **R**. **L** on 'C' st.
L on 8th, 1 block.
L on 'D'. Look **R** for creek.
R on path between creek and fence.

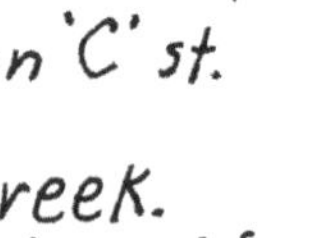

R on footbridge. **R** at end, through park.
L on 8th. **R** on California.

L on Laurelwood. Pass to right of info. board. Cross bridge
L on small path. Before bridge, **R** up trail. **R** at first fork, to Fir Street.

R at Street (5th). **L** on Pine.
Cross 4th. Veer **L** to cross bridge.
L on 3rd. **R** on Elm.
Cross Sterling, go **R**.
R on Oregon. **L** on Pine into Britt G.
- Down steps, back to parking lot.

-or- Up steps to info. board.
R on Zigler, easy 1 mile trail.
turn around at parking lot.

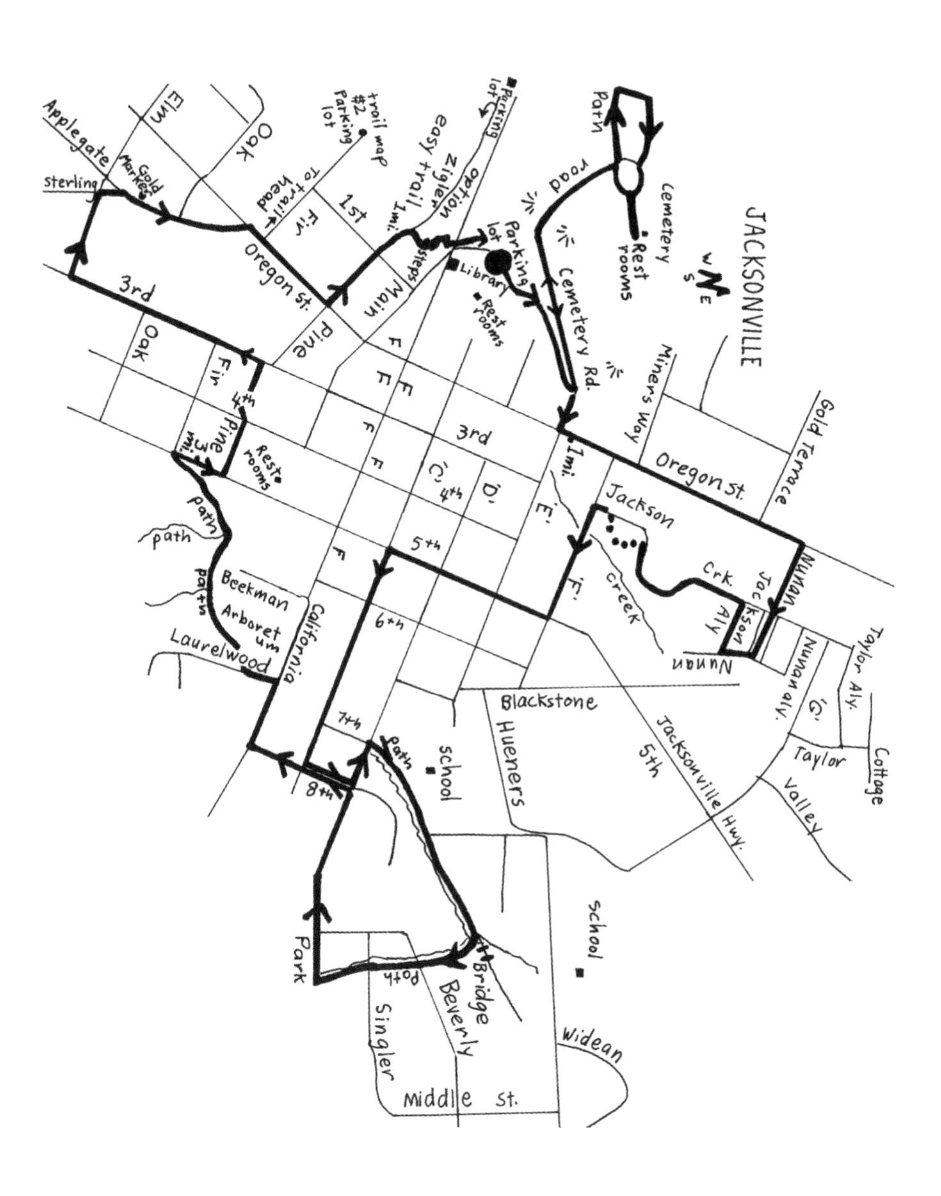
JACKSONVILLE
Applegate
Sterling
Gold Marker
Elm
Oak
To trail head
trail map #2 Parking lot
easy trail
Zigler
option
1 mi.
Parking lot
Fir
1st
Oregon St.
Main
steps
Library
Parking lot
Rest rooms
road
Path
Cemetery
Rest rooms
Cemetery Rd.
3rd
Oak
Pine
Fir
4th
Pine
3 mi.
Rest rooms
F
3rd
C
4th
D
E
1 mi.
Miners Way
Gold Terrace
Oregon St.
Jackson
Crk.
Jackson
Aly
Nunan
creek
5th
F
6th
path
path
path
Beekman
Arboretum
Laurelwood
California
7th
8th
Path
school
Blackstone
Hueners
5th
Jacksonville Hwy.
Nunan aly.
Taylor Aly.
G
Taylor
Cottage
Valley
Park
Path
Bridge
Beverly
Singler
Middle St.
school
Widean

JUNCTION CITY

Distances: *2.6, 3.4 or 6.2 miles. Flat.

Start/finish: E 6th Ave and Greenwood.
From I-5 exit 216 to Halsey. Follow signs to Junction City.
L on 6th, 1 block. **R** on Greenwood. Use free parking lot.

Walk to 6th, go **L**. Cross Juniper, go **R**.
L on W15th. **L** on Kalima.
R on 3rd, 1 block. **R** on Laurel.
L on 10th 1 block. **L** on Maple.

L on W5th. Cross Ivy, go **L**.
R on 9th, 1 block. **R** on Holly.
L on 3rd, 1 block. **L** on Greenwood.
(for 3.4 mi. end at 6th.)
*for 2.6 mi. START **L** on Greenwood.

395 Kalima

R on W 9th, 1 block. **R** on Front St.
L on E 6th, 1 block. **L** on Elm.
R on 14th, jog **R** then **L** on Dane.
Walk facing the traffic.
Go to #29361 Dane, the big yellow and green house.
Turn around here.

Depot
5th and Holly

L on Deal st.
L on 9th, curves **R** onto Alder.
L on E 3rd. **L** on Dorsa St.
At Bergstrom Park, veer right on path past tennis courts.
L at the street (6th).
L at Greenwood to end.

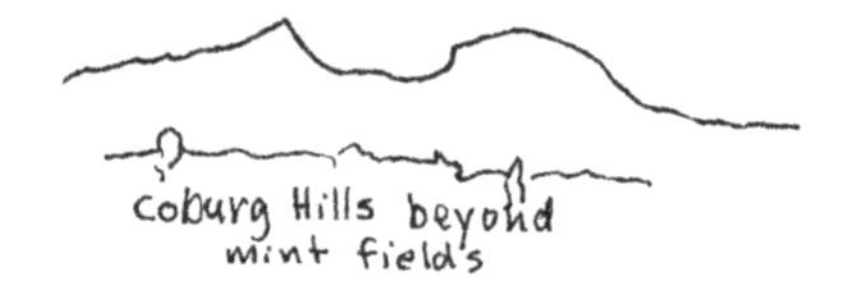

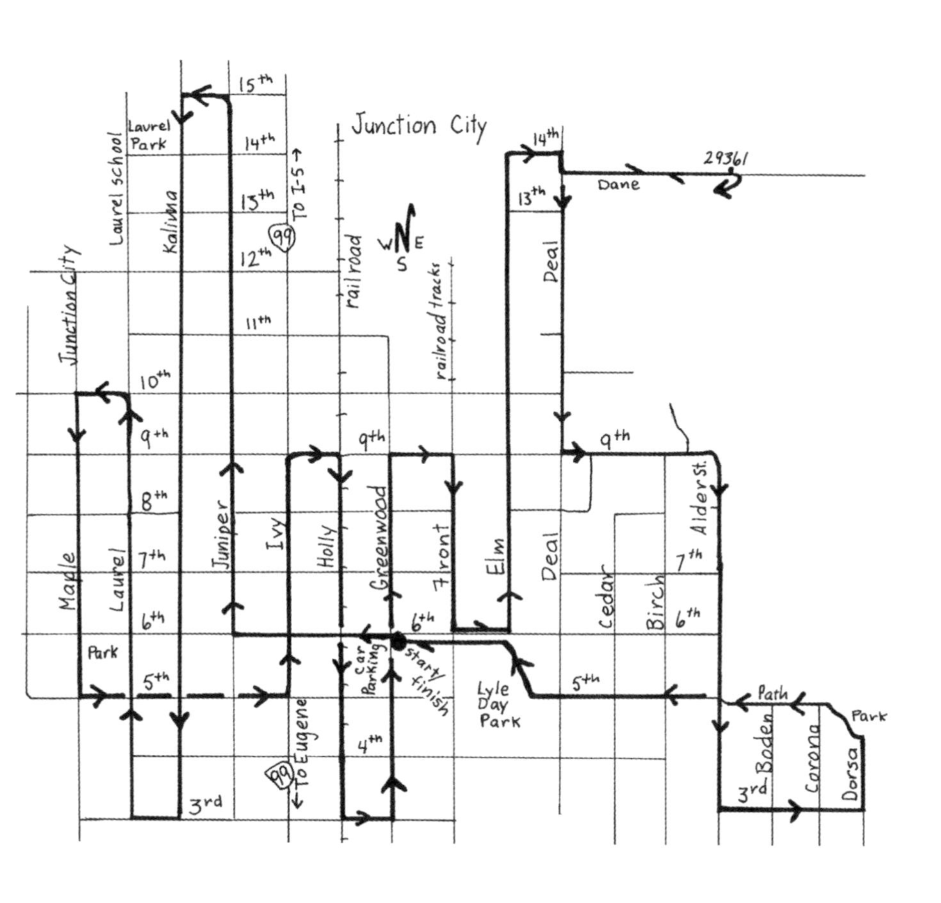
Junction City
15th
14th
13th
12th
11th
10th
9th
8th
7th
6th
5th
4th
3rd
Laurel Park
Laurel school
Kalima
Junction City
To I-5 →
99
railroad
W N E S
railroad tracks
14th
13th
29361
Dane
Deal
9th
Maple
Laurel
Juniper
Ivy
Holly
Greenwood
Front
Elm
Deal
Cedar
Birch
Alder St.
7th
6th
Park
Car Parking
start/finish
Lyle Day Park
5th
Path
Park
Boden
Corona
Dorsa
3rd
99
To Eugene
↓

KLAMATH FALLS Directions

Arrive by Amtrak train at Oak and Spring. Walk toward street. **R** on Spring. **L** on Main St.

Nearest lodging:

- Maverick Motel, .4 mile away 1220 Main. 541-882-6688
- One mile away, Econo Lodge, 75 Main. 541-884-7735 Quality Inn, 100 Main. 541-882-8795. Ask for a ride, or walk.

Arrive by car to Downtown: From the north on 97, take Business 97. **R** on Main to Klamath Co. Museum.

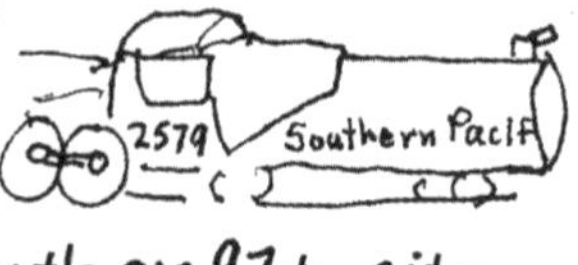

From the south on 97 to city center, exit toward visitor center, on to Main.

For history on downtown and 1945 deaths by balloon, ask at the Klamath Co. Museum.

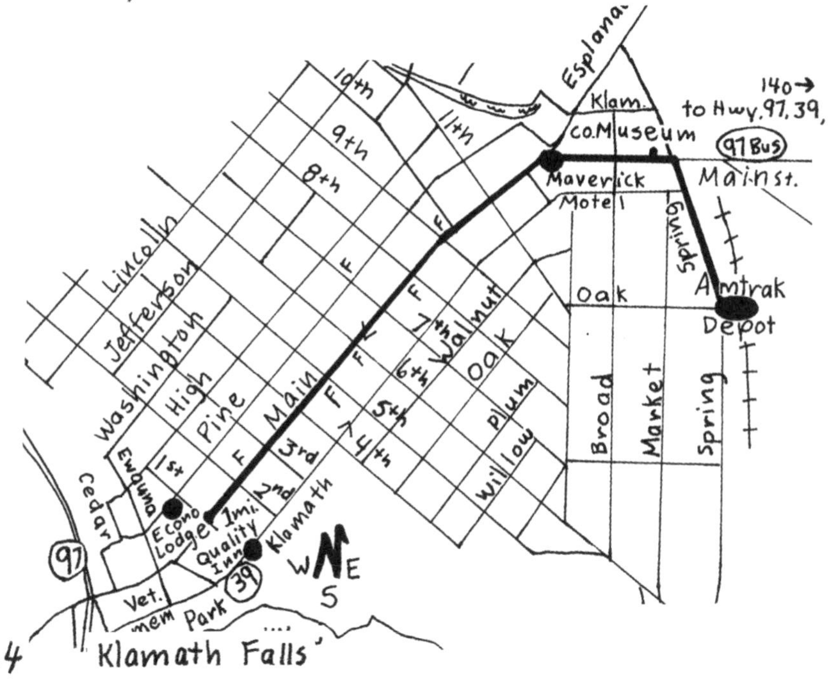

OC&E WOODS LINE

Klamath Falls

Distance: 100 miles of converted railroad bed. First 7 miles paved, 88 miles fine gravel.

Directions to city trailheads:
From city center, take Hwy 39 towards Reno, Lakeview.

Trailhead 1 → **R** on Washburn Way
L on Crosby. **L** at Avalon.
Trailhead 2 → **R** on Wiard to Park.
Trailhead 3 → **R** on 39, toward Reno.
After Hager Way, **R** to parking lot.

For entire map, visit www.oregonstateparks.org

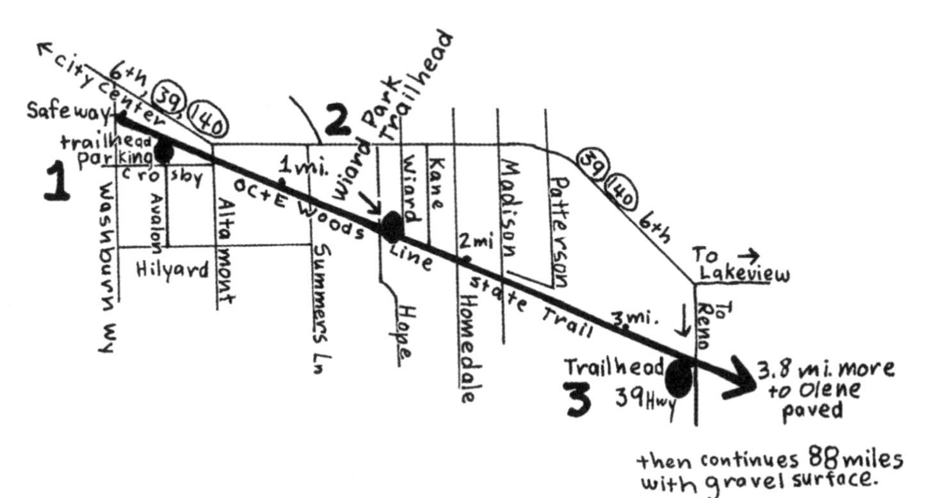

The world could, and would, walk this trail if there were accommodations every 10-15 miles!

DOWNTOWN and TRAILS

Klamath Falls

Distances: 2.5 mi., up to 8.2 miles. Flat.

Start finish: Klamath Co. Museum, at Main and Spring Streets. Museum has a Historic Downtown brochure and restrooms. Open Tu-Sa. 9-5.

With your back to Museum entry, **R** on Main St. At traffic light, cross toward left, continue. After Quality Inn, use cross walk to traffic island. At end, **L** across street to path in park.

Straight to lake. **R** along lake. Curves uphill, use sidewalk on right side. Cross street, Main, and go **L**. Pass Favell Museum. **L** on Riverside, on right side. At house 234, return to Favell Museum.

Options from Favell Museum:

1. Link River Trail, past the Museum. 3 miles out and back.
2. Klamath Falls Wingwatcher Trail. Enter across from Museum. 2.6 mile loop around pond.
3. Return to start, use left side of Main St., 2.5 mi. total.

Combine all options for 8.2 miles. Return to start on left side of Main Street.

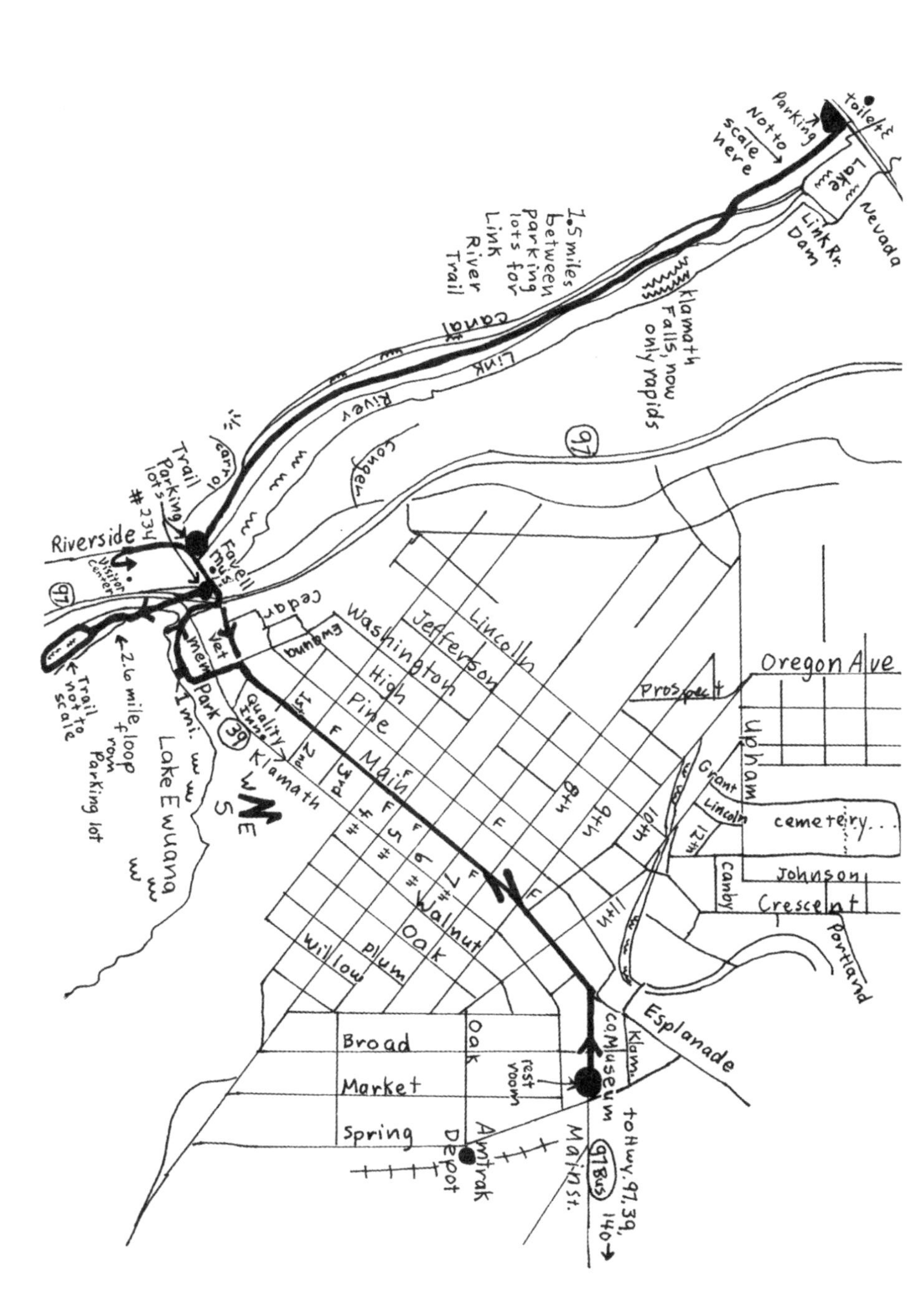
Parking
Not to scale here
toilet
Lake
Nevada
Link Rr. Dam
1.5 miles between parking lots for Link River Trail
Klamath Falls, now only rapids
Canal
Link River
Conger
Carr
Trail Parking lots # 234
Riverside
Visitor Center
Favell mus.
Cedar
Ewauna
Washington
Jefferson
Lincoln
High
Pine
Main
Vet mem Park
Quality Inne
1 mi.
2.6 mile loop from Parking lot
Trail not to scale
Lake Ewuana
Klamath
Oregon Ave
Prospect
Upham
Grant
Lincoln
cemetery
Johnson
Crescent
Canby
Portland
Walnut
Oak
Plum
Willow
Esplanade
Broad
Market
Spring
Oak
rest room
Co. Museum
Klam.
Amtrak Depot
Main St.
97 Bus
to Hwy. 97, 39, 140

CEMETERY & CHURCHES

Klamath Falls

Distance: 1.3 mi. 105 ft. ascent. 3.1 mi. 260 ft.

Directions to start:
From 39 or 97, exit to city center.
South (opposite hill) on 7th.
R on Oak. Park here, all day free.

Start/finish: Oak St. between 6th and 7th.
On Oak, **R** on 6th
R on Pine. (for 1.3 mi., **L** on 8th
(**R** on High. See ✱ .)
L on 11th. **R** on Grant, into
Linkville cemetery. Follow road
R around cemetery.
Pass flag, exit downhill.

Laws graves

exit

L on Canby. **R** on Crescent.
Cross Alameda, across bridge
onto Washington, on right side.
L on 10th, **L** on High, walk on
left side, it is easier.

✱ **R** on 5th. For ease, use left side.
L on Washington.
L on Ewuana, 1 block.
R on High. **L** on Cedar.
L on Pine. (after viewing front
of white Victorian house on **R**)

R on 3rd.
L on Klamath St.
R on 5th.
L on Oak to end.

Raglund
theater

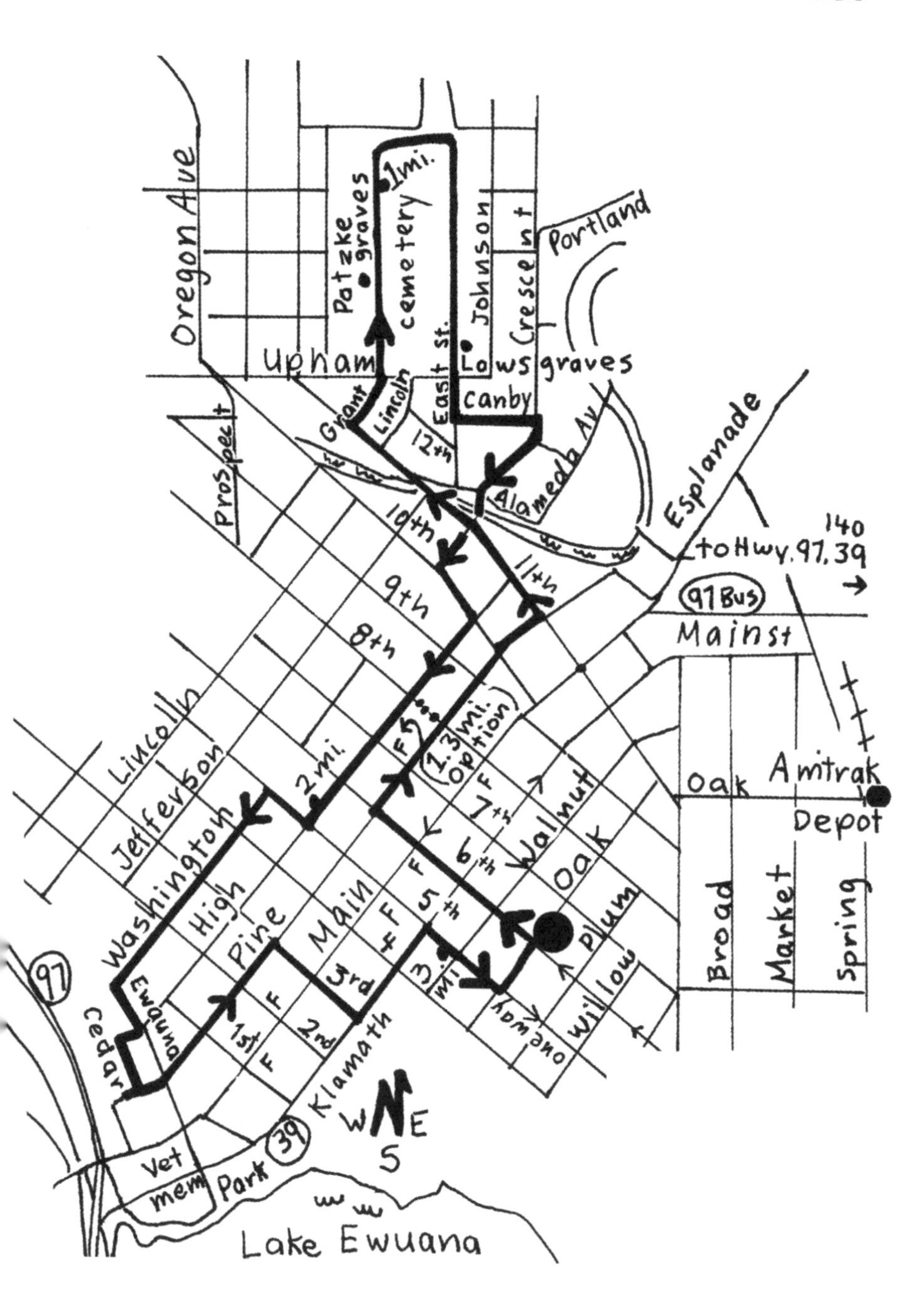
Oregon Ave
Patzke graves
cemetery
1mi.
Johnson
Crescent
Portland
Upham
East st.
Lows graves
Canby
Grant
Lincoln
12th
Prospect
Alameda Av
Esplanade
10th
11th
140
to Hwy. 97, 39
97 Bus
Main st
9th
8th
Lincoln
Jefferson
Washington
2mi.
1.3 mi. Option
7th
6th
Walnut
Oak
Amitrak Depot
Oak
High
Pine
Main
5th
4
3rd
Plum
Broad
Market
Spring
97
Cedar
Ewauna
1st
2nd
3mi
one way
Willow
Klamath
39
W
N
E
S
Vet mem Park
Lake Ewuana

HEALING GARDEN Lebanon

Distance: 2.5 miles. Flat.

Start/finish: Rose St. and So. 6th
From I-5, take exit 228.
R on So. 6th to Rose. Park on street.

On Rose St., walk past park building and tennis courts, pass the park. Cross 5th.
R on Main St., 1 block.
L on Vine, 1 block.
L on Park, straight through Pioneer Cemetery.

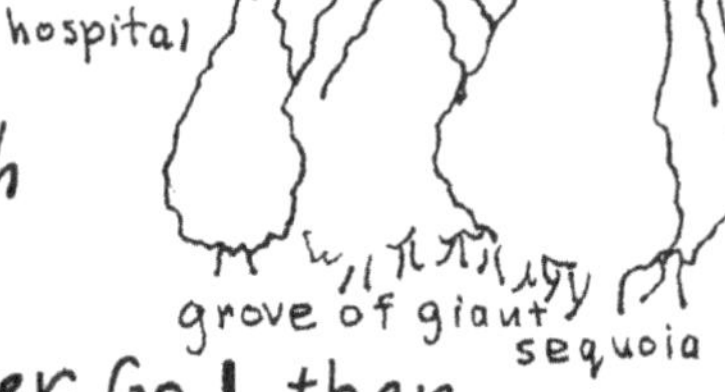

Healing Gardens

Cross Wheeler. Go **L** then **R** on Eaton. At the end of Eaton, cross railroad tracks. Pass between 2 big gray buildings.
Elkin's Mill c.1872. See reader board next to mill.
Straight to sidewalk.
R around big brick building, Passing Redwood Grove.

Cross street. Go **L** then **R** into parking lot. Stay **R** through the parking lots to hospital back entrance. Enter hospital, go straight down hall to Healing Garden, then Atrium Sculpture Garden.

Return to Wheeler the way you came. **R** on Wheeler, on to Milton.
Curves **L** to 2nd.
Curves **L** to Academy.
R on 2nd.
R on Rose to end.

Pond by hospital Lebanon

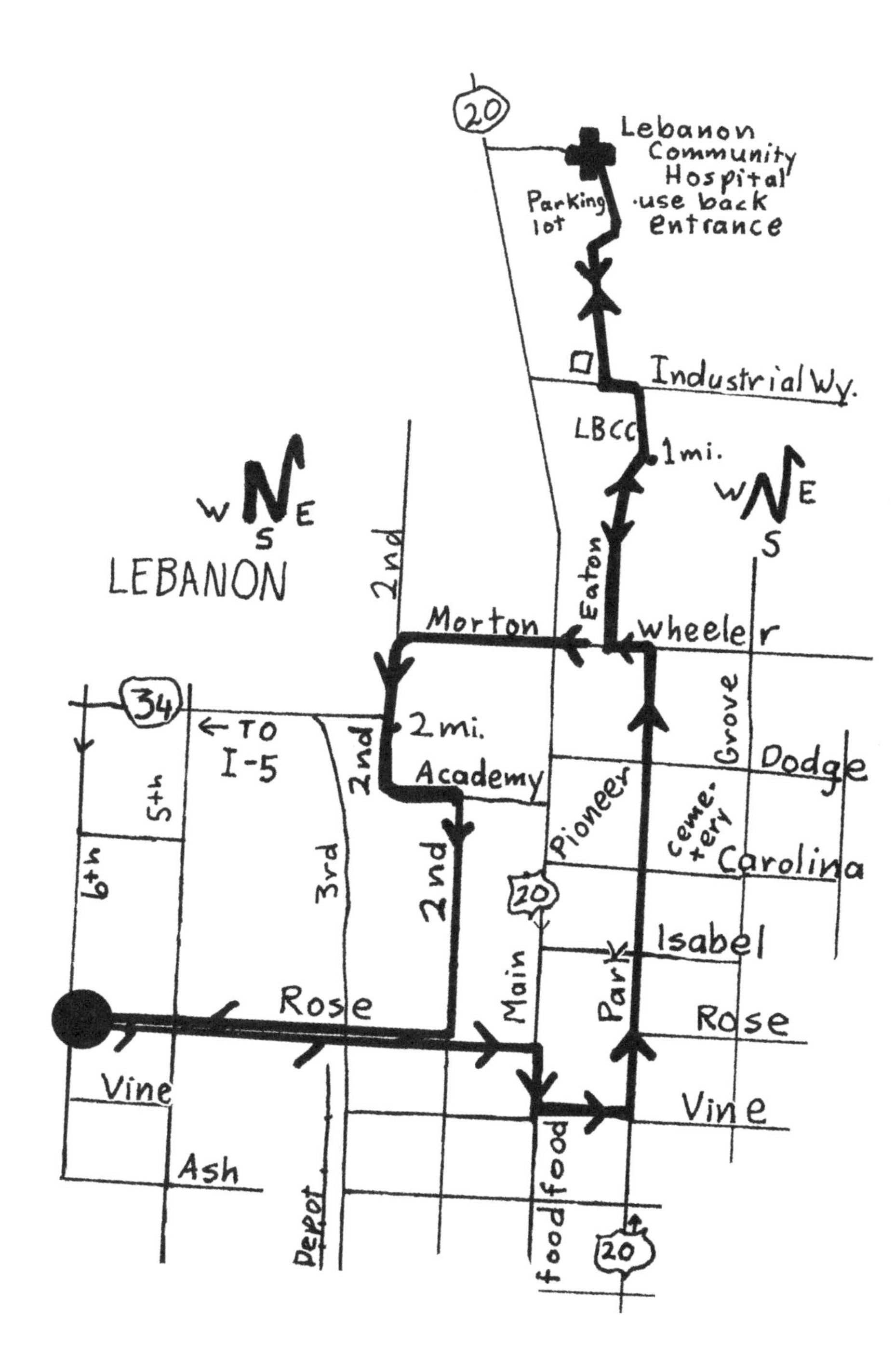

20
Lebanon Community Hospital
Parking lot
use back entrance
Industrial Wy.
LBCC
1mi.
W N E S
LEBANON
2nd
Eaton
Morton
Wheeler
34
← TO I-5
2mi.
2nd
Academy
Grove
Dodge
Pioneer
cemetery
Carolina
5th
6th
3rd
2nd
20
Isabel
Main
Park
Rose
Rose
Vine
Vine
Ash
Depot
food
food
20

CLASSIC DOWNTOWN

Lebanon

Distance: 3.5 mi. or 5 miles. Flat.

on Grant and 4th

Start/finish: Rose and So. 6th.
From I-5, take exit 228.
R on So. 6th to Rose. Park on street.

On 6th, your back to the park, go on 6th 2 blocks, cross Vine.
L on Ash St., 1 block.
R on 5th. **L** on Grant.
L on 3rd, pass depot.
R on Vine.
R on Main St.

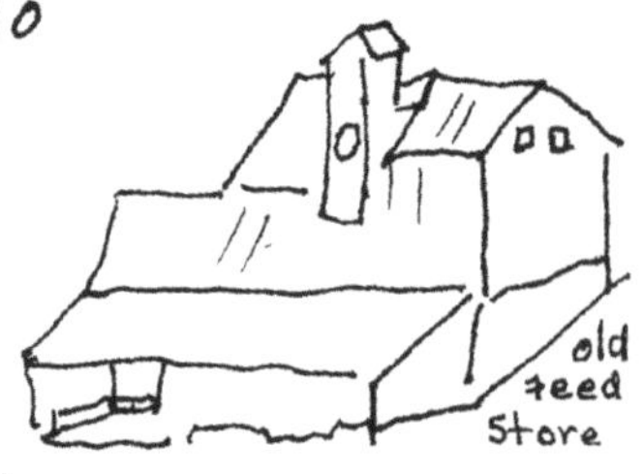

old feed Store

L on Oak, 1 block.
Cross Park St. Take diagonal path through park.
L on Grove, 1 block.
R on Williams.
L on Elmore.
R on Franklin.

Ash and 5th Church Christ

L on River, curves right.
Cross foot bridge.
L on Mountain River, 1 block.
L on Park. Cross Milton.
L on Milton, 1 block.
R on Filbert. **R** on Elmore, 1 block.
L on Eddie. **R** on Oak.
L on River. **L** on Grant.

916 River

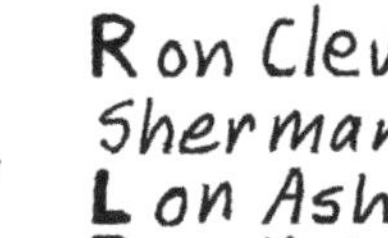

R on Cleveland, curves **L** to Sherman. **L** on Crescent.
L on Ash. **R** on Park. **L** on Isabell.
R on Main, 1 block.
L on Rose to 6th.

classic downtown

Lebanon

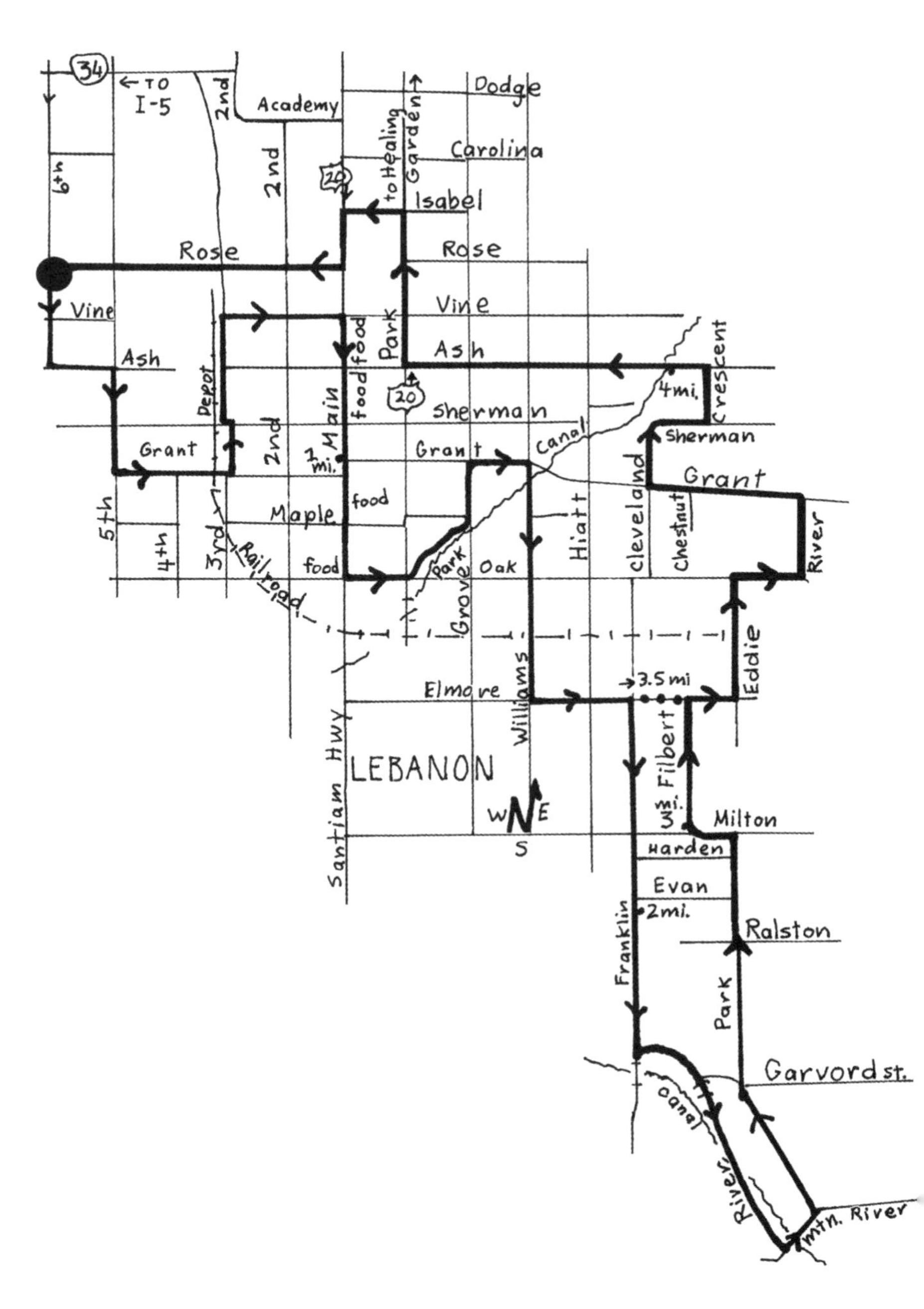
34
← TO I-5
6th
2nd
Academy
2nd
Dodge
Carolina
Isabel
to Healing Garden
20
Rose
Rose
Vine
Vine
Ash
Ash
Park
Depot
Main
food
food
20
Sherman
Grant
2nd
1 mi.
Grant
Canal
4 mi.
Crescent
Sherman
Grant
5th
4th
3rd
Maple
food
food
Railroad
Park
Grove
Oak
Hiatt
Cleveland
Chestnut
River
Eddie
Elmore
Williams
3.5 mi
Filbert
3 mi.
Santiam Hwy
LEBANON
W N E S
Milton
Harden
Evan
2 mi.
Franklin
Ralston
Park
Garvord st.
canal
River
Mtn. River

HISTORIC HOMES MEDFORD

Distance: 2.7 miles. Flat.

From I-5, Exit 27, to Barnett, turn toward Medford.
R on (99), Riverside Ave.
R on 10th (next street after 12th) for 1 block.
L on Tripp. **L** into free parking lot.

Start/finish: 9th st. and Almond parking lot.

Go to the river. **R** on the path. When you see the Red Lion Inn across the river, go **R** off river path, before next street (Jackson). Walk along Hawthorne Park.

R on Genesse. **L** on Main, 1 block.
L on Geneva. **R** on Sherman.
L on Stark.
R on Jackson, 1/2 block.
R on Crater Lake, 1 block.
R on Minnesota, 1 block.

L on Geneva. Cross Main St., go **R** to corner. **L** on Cottage.
L on Taylor. **L** on Myrtle.
R on Main.
R on Vancouver.
R on 9th.

Cross Cottage St.
Cross Tripp St. to sidewalk along street.
R down to bike path before crossing river, to finish.

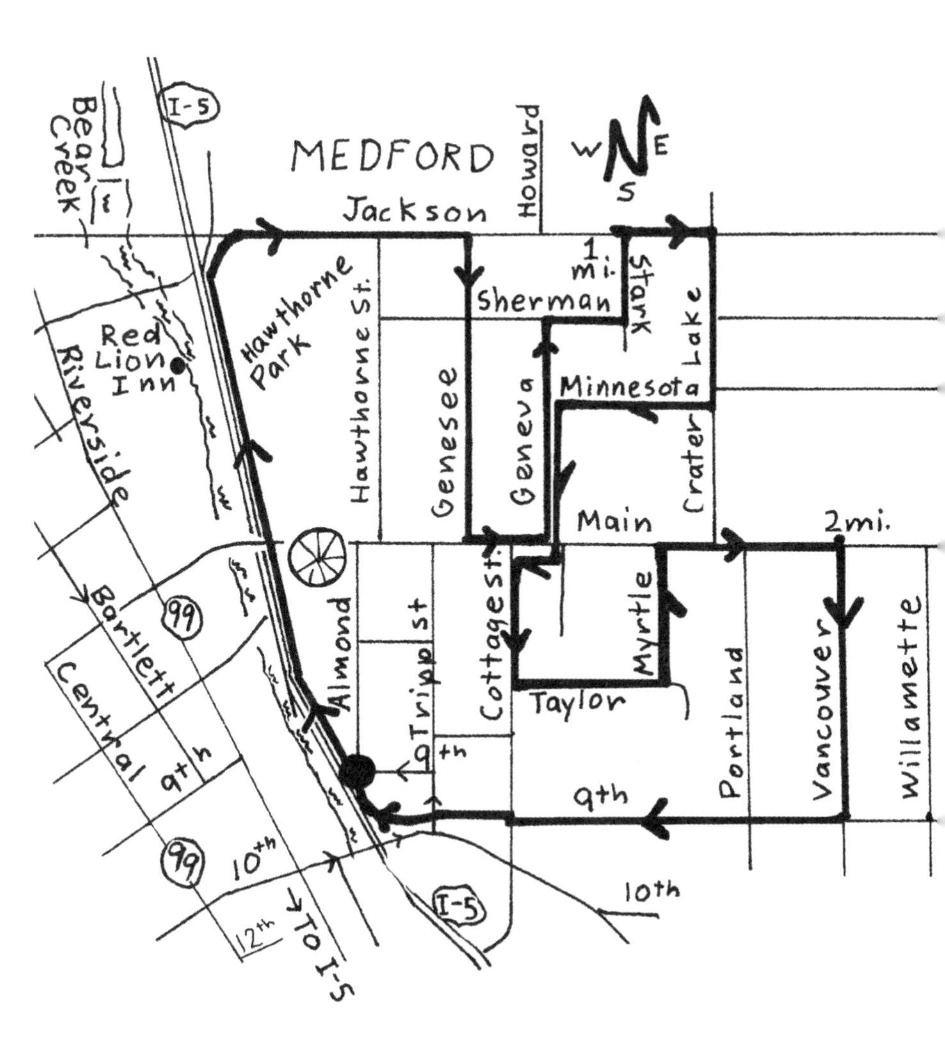

MEDFORD
I-5
Bear Creek
Jackson
Howard
W N E S
1 mi.
Sherman
Stark
Lake
Hawthorne Park
Hawthorne St.
Red Lion Inn
Riverside
Genesee
Geneva
Minnesota
Crater
Main
2mi.
Bartlett
Central
99
Almond
Tripp st
Cottage st.
Myrtle
Taylor
Portland
Vancouver
Willamette
9th
10th
12th
To I-5

Historic Downtown Medford

Distance: 2.5 miles. Flat.

Start/finish: 9th St. and Almond. Park by river.
From I-5, exit 27, to downtown on Barnett. **R** on 10th. **L** on Tripp. **L** on 9th to parking. (Free)

on Main St.

Cross the footbridge over the river.
R at street (Riverside), ½ block.
L on 9th. **R** on Front.
L on Main. At Holly St., Take the diagonal path through park, pass the statue. **R** on 8th.

Mcloughlin middle school

R on Oakdale, curves **R**. **R** on 2nd.
R on Grape.
R on 4th.
L on Ivy.
L on 6th.
L on Front, 1 block.

1915 US courthouse Built as a Post Office on 6th

R on 5th, 1 block.
R on Central, 1 ½ blocks.
L down Middleford Alley.
R at street (Riverside), 1 block.

Waverly Cottage 305 Grape

Zion Lutheran church

L on Main.
Cross bridge.
L after bridge.
L on bike path along river, back to foot bridge.
Or continue on the Medford Historic 'hood map.

old train depot

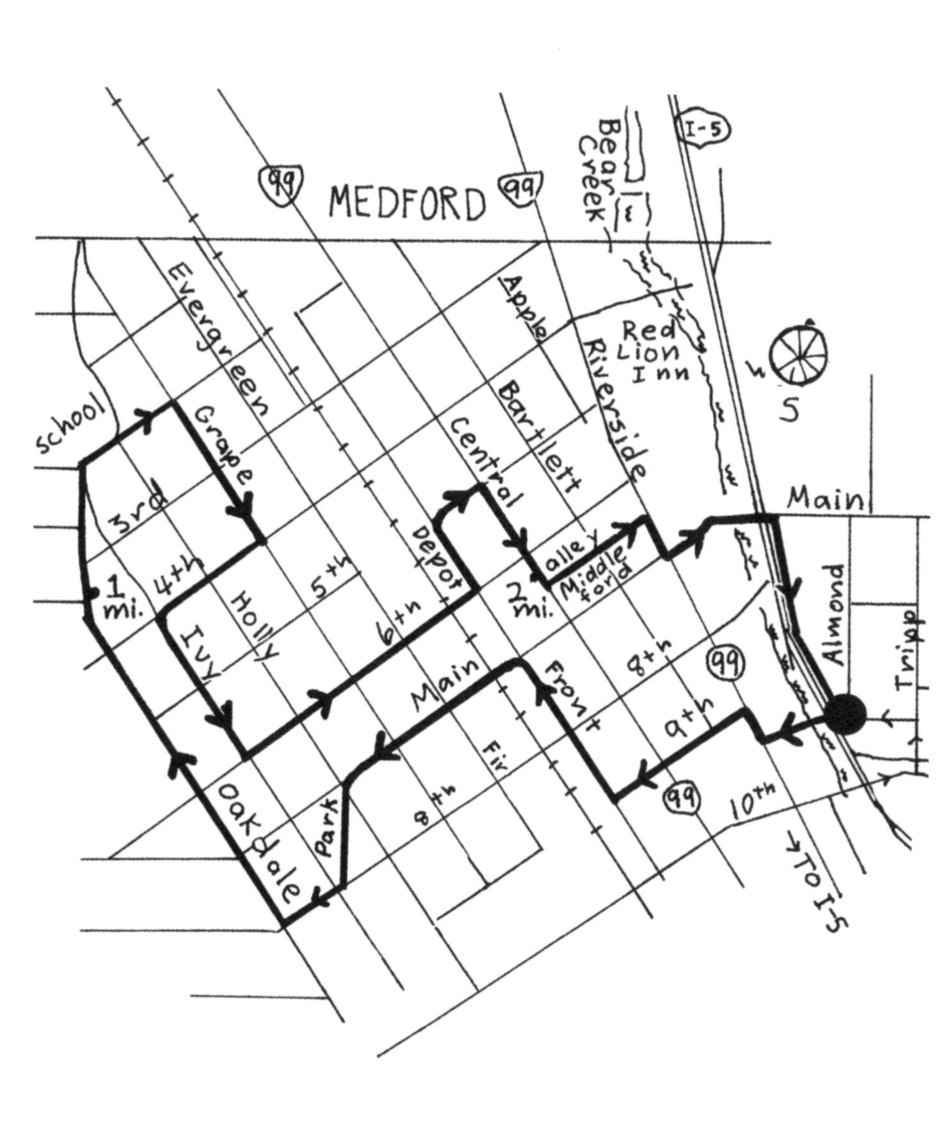
MEDFORD
99
99
I-5
Bear Creek
Red Lion Inn
Evergreen
Apple
Bartlett
Riverside
Central
Grape
School
3rd
4th
1 mi.
Holly
5th
Depot
6th
alley
Middle ford
2 mi.
Ivy
Main
Main
Front
8th
99
9th
Almond
Tripp
Fir
Oakdale
Park
8th
99
10th
To I-5
S

OREGON CITY

Directions to End of Oregon Trail center.
From I-5, north or south:

Merge onto I-205.
Exit 10 to Hwy. 213 toward Molalla.
R on Washington.
L into Oregon Tr. Ctr. parking lot.

Lodging: Rivershore Motel, 2 star, 1.5 mi. from Amtrak
1900 Clackamette, 1-800-443-7777.
Ask them for a ride.

Bus to Portland: At 11th and Main St.
Departs every 15 minutes,
40-minute ride. $2.00.

History: All on the Willamette Falls map.

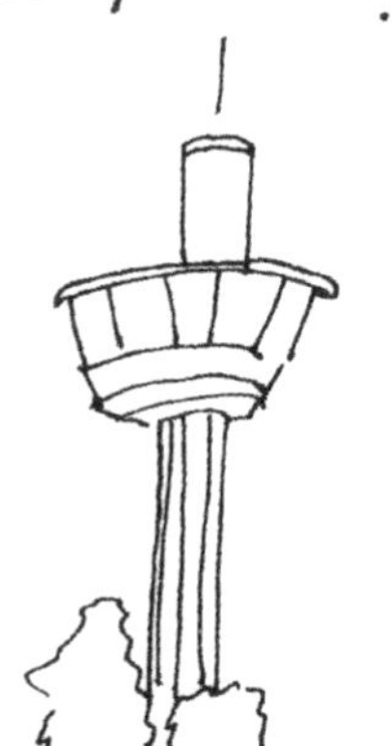

- End of Oregon Trail center
  Open Tu-Sa 11-4 $7 includes
- Oregon Territorial Museum
  211 Tumwater Tu-Sa. 11-4
- Stevens Crawford House
  6th and Morrison W-Sa. 12-4

Courthouse at Main and 8th.
In the entrance hall, find San Francisco's original plat, filed here, the first courthouse on the west coast.

Online at www.ci.oregon-city.or.us
click on "about", then "history".

OREGON CITY

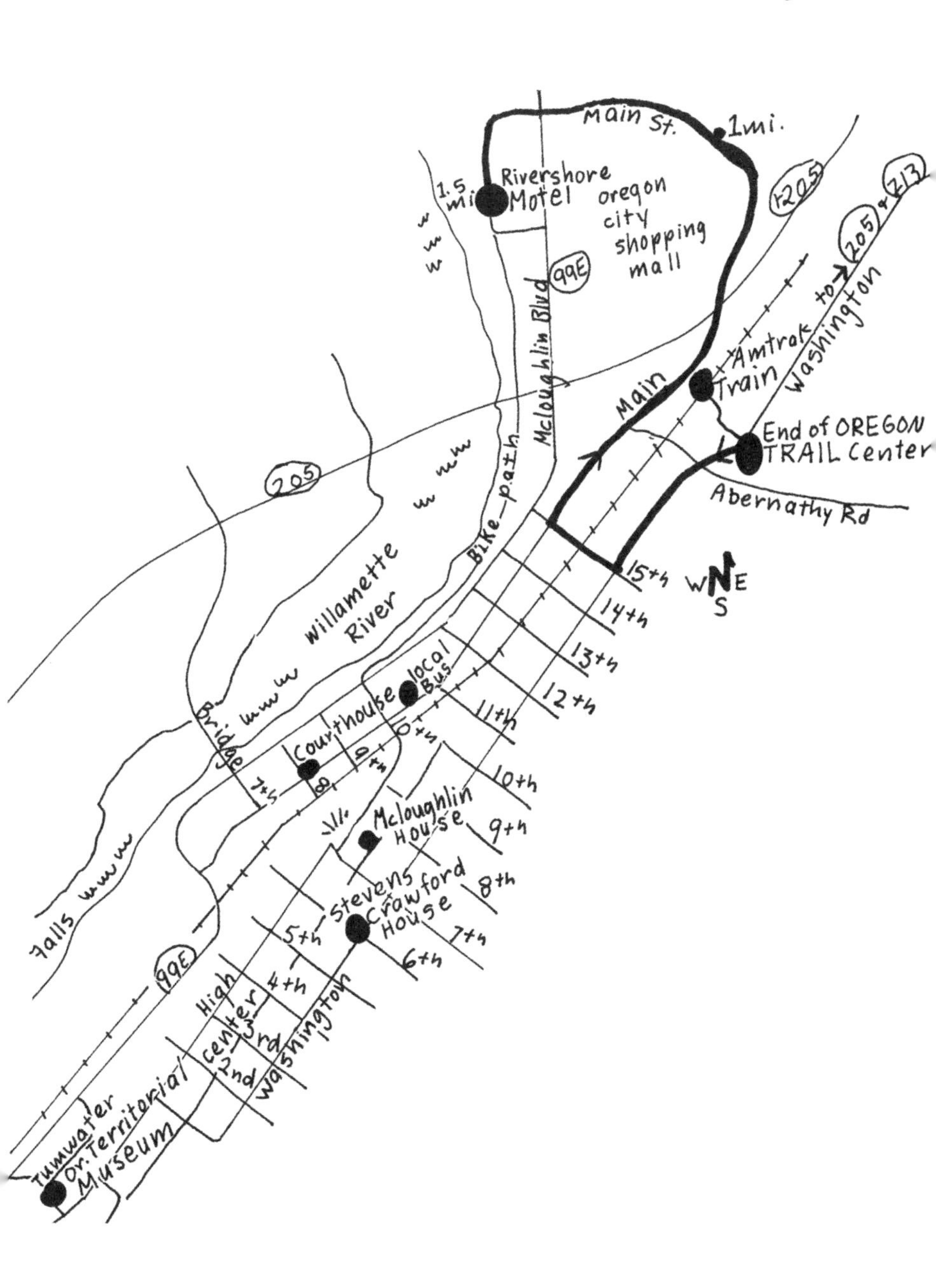

Main St.
1mi.
1.5 mi
Rivershore Motel
oregon city shopping mall
I205
205 & 213
99E
Mcloughlin Blvd
Amtrak Train
Washington to 205
Main
End of OREGON TRAIL Center
Abernathy Rd
205
Bike path
Willamette River
15th
14th
13th
12th
11th
10th
9th
8th
7th
6th
5th
4th
3rd
2nd
W N E S
local Bus
Courthouse
Bridge
Mcloughlin House
Stevens Crawford House
Falls
99E
High
center
Washington
Tumwater
Or. Territorial Museum

WILLAMETTE FALLS

OREGON CITY

Distance: 3.4 mi. or 5 mi. flat with elevator

Start/finish: Oregon Trail Center Parking lot

L on Washington St.

R on 14th. **L** on Main St.

R on 7th, on left side of street.

Cross bridge.

L on Mill st. right after bridge, through parking lot.

At the driver check-in, take path to left of building, by stop sign.

Anchor by Willamette locks

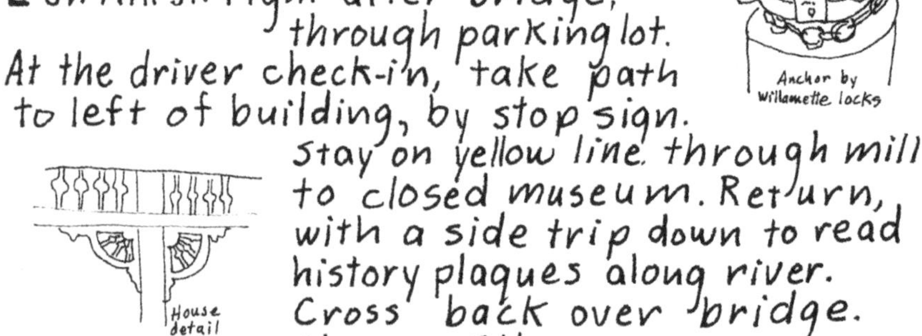

House detail

Stay on yellow line through mill to closed museum. Return, with a side trip down to read history plaques along river.

Cross back over bridge.

Stay on 7th.

At 7th and Railroad, into tunnel.

Up free elevator or stairs on left.

R at top, onto path. (for 3.4 mi. walk, **L** to 7th. **R** on 7th. **L** on Center. See * below.

McLoughlin Promenade, view of Willamette Falls

Through parking lot to Oregon Territory Museum. (restrooms)

From Tumwater St. **L** on So. 2nd.

R on Center, 1/2 block.

L up and onto Adams.

R on 2nd, 1 block. **L** on Jefferson.

L down alley after 4th

R at street (JA Adams) **L** on 7th.

Bush House

204 Jefferson

* **R** on Center, 1 block. **R** on 8th.

L on Jefferson. **L** on 12th, 1 block.

R on J. A. Adams. **L** on 15th, 1 block.

R on Washington to finish.

church top

OREGON CITY

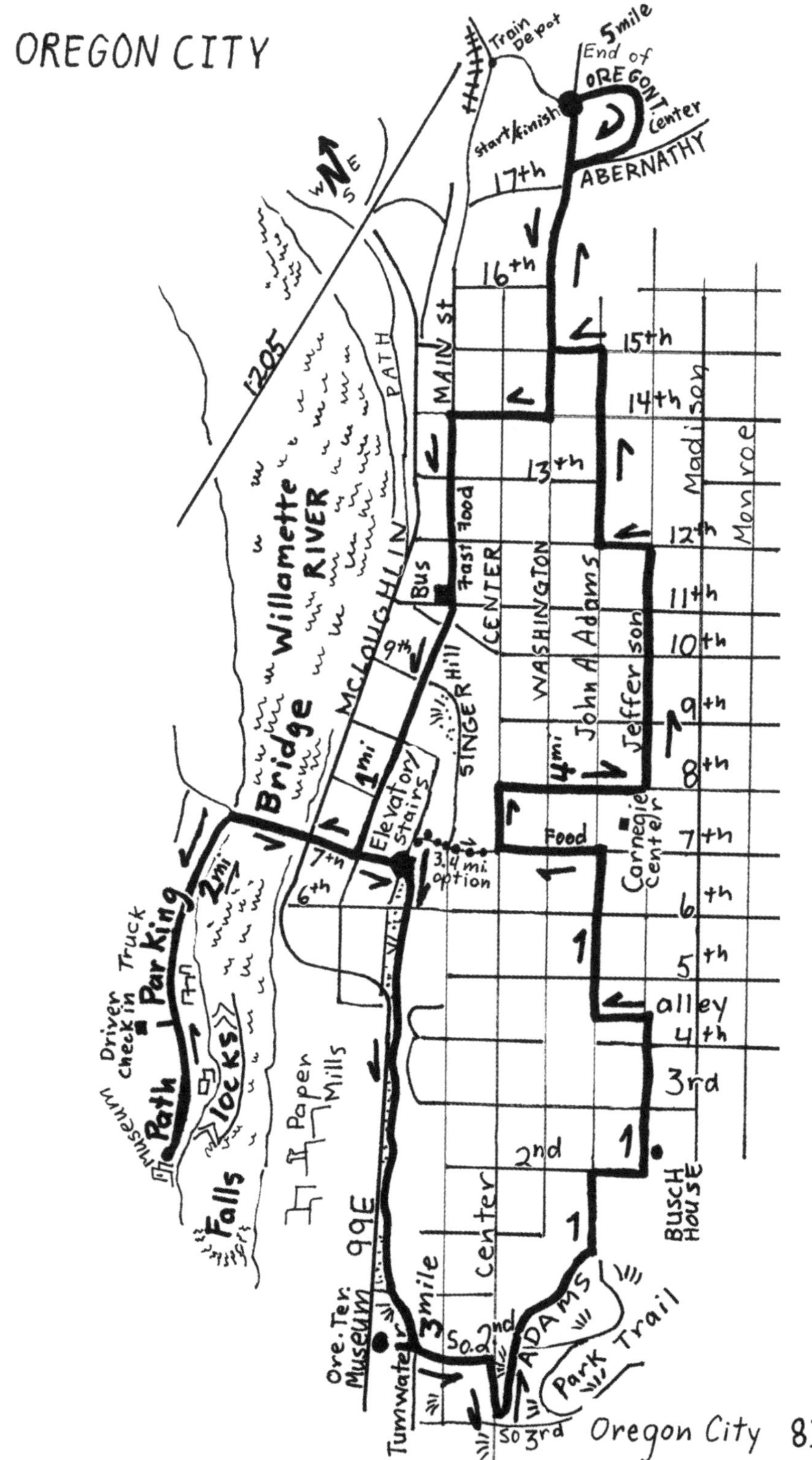
Train Depot
5 mile
End of
OREGON T. center
start/finish
ABERNATHY
17th
16th
15th
14th
13th
12th
11th
10th
9th
8th
7th
6th
5th
alley
4th
3rd
2nd
I-205
Willamette RIVER
PATH
MAIN St
MCLOUGHLIN
Bus
Fast Food
CENTER
WASHINGTON
John Adams
Jefferson
Madison
Monroe
SINGER Hill
Elevator/stairs
1 mi
4 mi
Food
Carnegie Center
3.4 mi option
Bridge
2 mi
Truck Parking
Driver check in
Path
locks
Museum
Falls
Paper Mills
99E
Center
BUSCH HOUSE
3 mile
Ore. Ter. Museum
Tumwater
So. 2nd
ADAMS
Park Trail
So 3rd

TOP TIER TREK

Distance: 3.1 mi. or 6 mi. 440 ft. elevation gain

Start/finish: Oregon Trail Center parking lot.
L on Washington.
L on 15th, 1 block. **R** on Adams.
L on 12th. **R** on Jackson.
L on 8th. **L** on Taylor.
R on 10th, 1 block. **R** on Pierce.

1900 ERICKSON HOUSE

L on 8th, 1 block.
R on Buchanan.
R on Division, 1/2 block.
L on Warren.
R on Roosevelt.
L on Molalla. **R** on Pleasant, turns into Molalla.

R on Holmes. **R** on Belle, into park. **L** at fork. **L** on Linn.
R on Harding, curves left.
R on Barclay. **R** on Brighton.
L on Creed. Down trail on left.

Emerge on J. Adams St.
R on Adams.
R on 10th, 1 block.
L on Jefferson, 1 block.
L on 11th, 1 block.
R on Adams.

L on 15th.
R on Washington to finish.

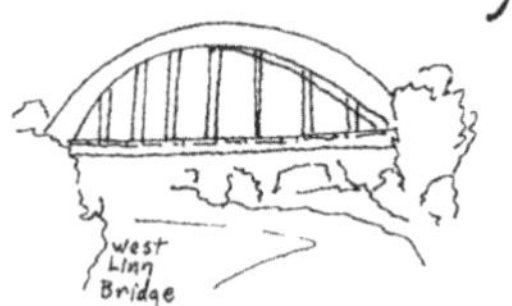

statues near library.

OREGON CITY

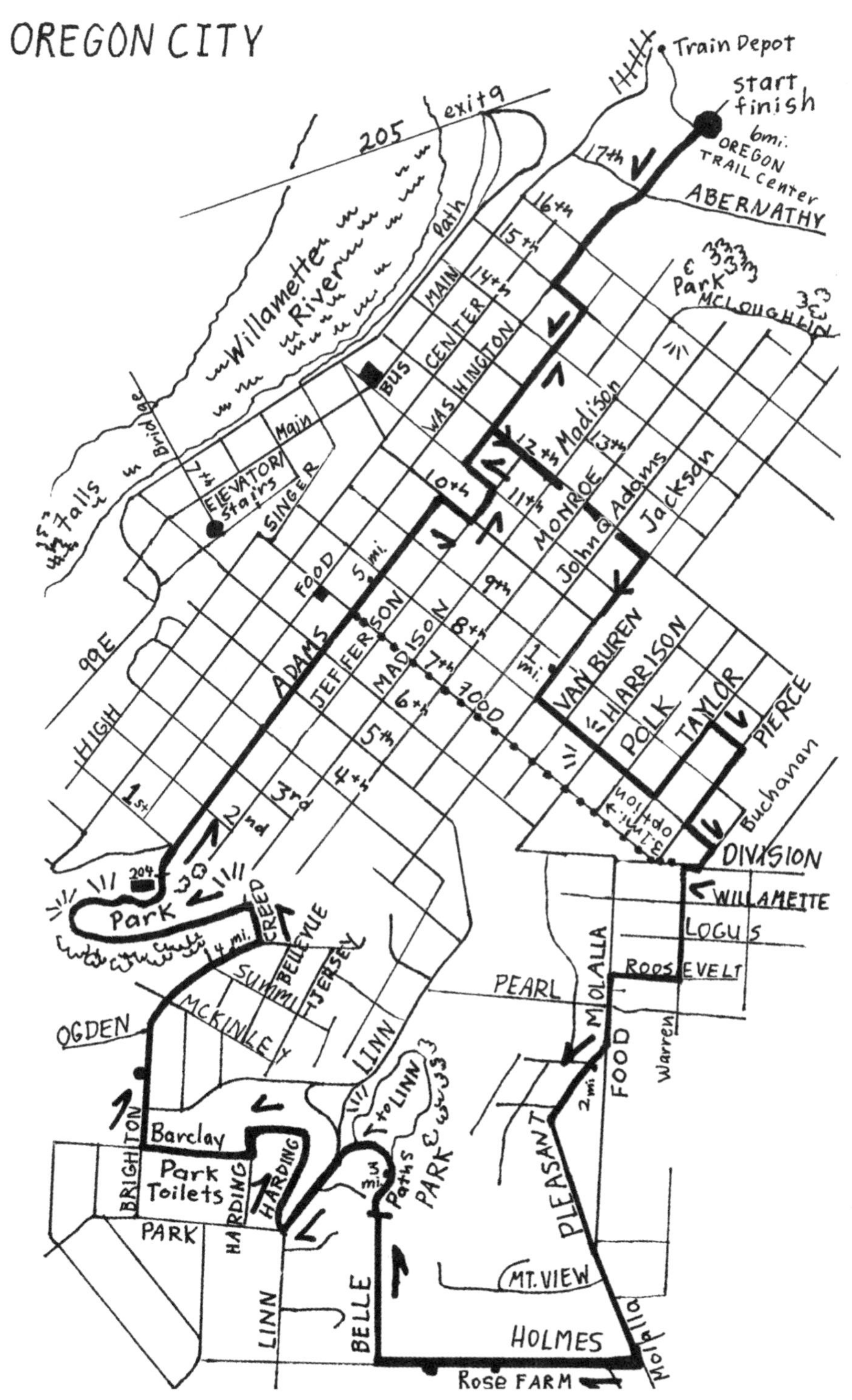

Train Depot
start finish
6mi. OREGON TRAIL Center
ABERNATHY
17th
16th
15th
14th
13th
12th
11th
10th
9th
8th
7th
6th
5th
4th
3rd
2nd
1st
205
exit 9
Willamette River
Path
Bridge
Falls
Main
ELEVATOR/ Stairs
7th
SINGER
BUS
MAIN
CENTER
WASHINGTON
Madison
MONROE
John Q Adams
Jackson
Park
MCLOUGHLIN
FOOD
5 mi.
ADAMS
JEFFERSON
MADISON
1 mi.
VAN BUREN
HARRISON
POLK
TAYLOR
PIERCE
Buchanan
7000
3.1 mi. option
DIVISION
WILLAMETTE
LOGUS
ROOSEVELT
PEARL
MOLALLA
FOOD
Warren
99E
HIGH
204
Park
4 mi.
CREED
BELLEVUE
SUMMIT
JERSEY
MCKINLEY
LINN
OGDEN
Barclay
BRIGHTON
Park Toilets
HARDING
PARK
to LINN
3 mi.
Paths
PARK
2 mi.
PLEASANT
MT. VIEW
HOLMES
BELLE
Rose FARM
Molalla

RIVER VIEWS

Distance: 3 mi. or 5.3 mi. flat or 252 ft. elevation

Start/finish: Oregon Trail Center Parking lot

L on Washington st. **R** on 15th.
R on Main. Curves left.
R through Clackamus Park car parking lot.
L on path along river. Pass motel. Stay on bike path to stop light.
L on 10th at stop light.
R on Main st.

(for 3 miles, **L** on Main st.
R on 12th. **L** on Adams.
L on 15th. **R** on Washington.)

west Linn Bridge

At Main and 8th go into Clackamus Co. Courthouse. Find the original plat of San Francisco on wall.

L on 7th into tunnel. Up free elevator or stairs on left. **L** to 7th. **R** on 7th.
R on Washington, 1 block.
L on 6th. **R** on Jefferson, 1 block.
L on 5th, 1 block. **L** on Madison, 1 block.
R on 6th, 2 blocks.

L on J.A. Adams, 1 block.
R on 7th, 2 blocks.
L on Van Buren, 1 block.
L on 8th, 1 block

Municipal Elevator

R on Jackson, 1 block. **L** on 9th, 1 block.
L on J.A. Adams, 1 block **R** on 8th, 1 block.
L on Monroe, 1 block. **R** on 7th, 2 blocks.
R on Jefferson, 1 block.

Free tour McLoughlin House W-Sun 10-4 715 center

L on 8th. **R** on Center, 1 block.
R on 9th. **L** on Jefferson.
L on 12th. **R** on Adams.
L on 15th. **R** on Washington to end.

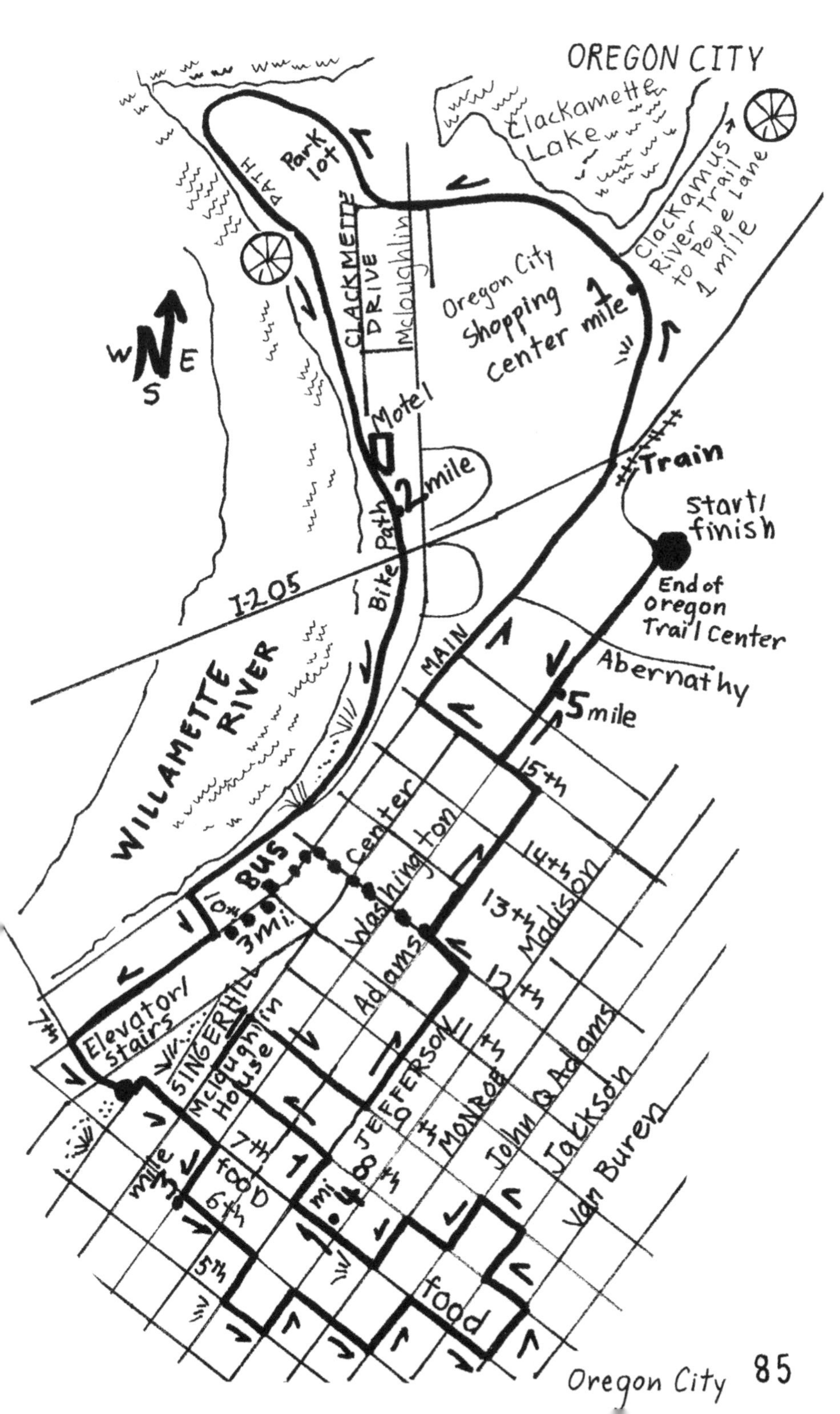

OREGON CITY
Clackamette Lake
Clackamus River Trail to Pope Lane 1 mile
Park lot
PATH
CLACKMETTE DRIVE
Mcloughlin
Oregon City Shopping center
1 mile
Motel
2 mile
Bike Path
Train
Start/ finish
End of oregon Trail Center
I-205
WILLAMETTE RIVER
MAIN
Abernathy
5 mile
15th
14th
13th
Madison
Center
Washington
BUS
10th
3 Mi.
Adams
12th
Elevator/ Stairs
7th
SINGERHILL
Mcloughlin House
JEFFERSON
11th
9th
MONROE
John Q Adams
Jackson
Van Buren
7th
8th
food
6th
mile 3
mi. 4
5th
food
W
N
E
S

PORTLAND

Directions to Union Station start point.

- From the south: Exit 299B toward Beaverton, on I-405 Exit 2B toward Everest, on 14th Av. **R** on Everett. **L** on Broadway **R** on Irvine. **L** on 6th.
- From the north: Exit 302A toward Broadway, Across the bridge. **L** on Irving. **L** on 6th.

Parking in garages near Union station.

Lodging: Close to Union Station there are many, Here are three.

- Benson Hotel, luxury (.6 mi.)
  309 SW Broadway
  1-888-523-6760
- Ace Hotel. Budget hip. (.7 mi.)
  1022 SW Stark
  1-503-228-2277
- Hostel and Guesthouse (.8 mi.)
  425 NW 18th.
  1-888-777-0067
- The Mark Spencer Hotel
  409 SW 11th good value
  1-800-548-3934 (.7 mi.)

Taxis are at Union station or call 1-503-227-1234.

Historical information available at:

- www.pdxhistory.com
- Visitor center downtown at Morrison and 6th.

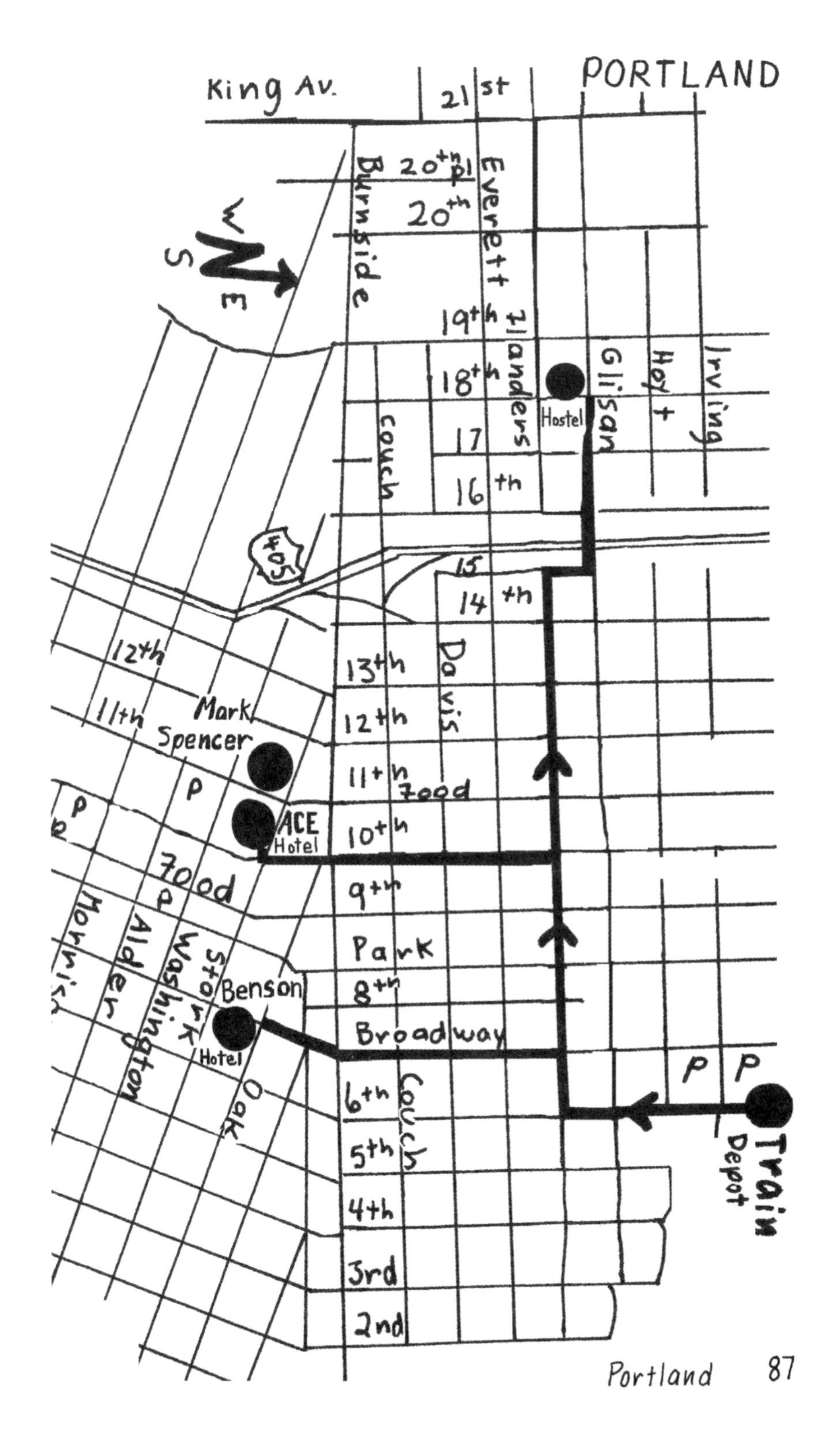
PORTLAND
King Av.
21st
20th pl
20th
19th
18th
17
16th
15
14th
13th
12th
11th
10th
9th
Park
8th
Broadway
6th
5th
4th
3rd
2nd
Burnside
Everett
Flanders
Glisan
Hoyt
Irving
Couch
Davis
Hostel
405
12th
11th
Mark
Spencer
ACE
Hotel
Yood
Yood
Morrison
Alder
Washington
Stark
Oak
Benson
Hotel
P
Train
Depot
W
N
S
E

HISTORIC IRVINGTON PORTLAND

Distances: * 2 mi. flat from Tillamook and NE 15th Ave.
▲ 3.7 mi. flat, from NE Holladay and NE 9th.
6.1 mi. flat, from Train Depot, Union Station.

Start/finish from Union Station, train depot.
With your back to the front door of Union Station,
L to corner. **L** to steps. Go up.
Straight to river. **R** on river path.
L across railroad tracks.
L at shiny steel sculptures.
Cross bridge over river.

Steel sculptures

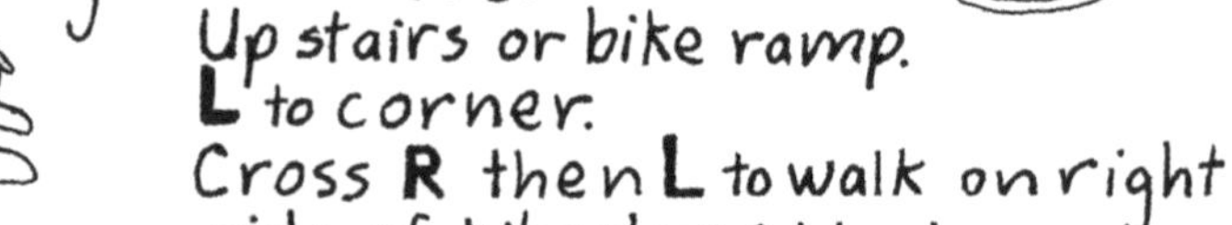

Up stairs or bike ramp.
L to corner.
Cross **R** then **L** to walk on right side of Wheeler, 1 block.
R on Holladay St. (Light Rail).

yard art

(▲ 3.7 mi. starts here.)
L on 9th. **R** on Tillamook St.
L on 14th. (* 2 mi. start/finish)
R on Knott. **R** on NE 24th, 1 block.
L on Brazee St. **R** on 28th 1 block.
R on Thompson. **L** on 25th 1 block.

R on Tillamook 1 block. **L** on 24th 1 block.
R on Hancock, 1 block.
L on Tillamook.

L on 15th. **R** on Broadway 1 block.
L on 14th. **R** on Halsey. **L** on 9th.
R on Holladay (▲ 3.7 ends here).
L on Wheeler. At next corner, cross NE Oregon St.
R across Interstate. **R** down to river, cross bridge.

eye brow window

R at steel sculptures. **L** after tracks.
R along street (Naito).
L at Big Ped-xing sign, up to bridge.
Cross to Union Station.

PORTLAND

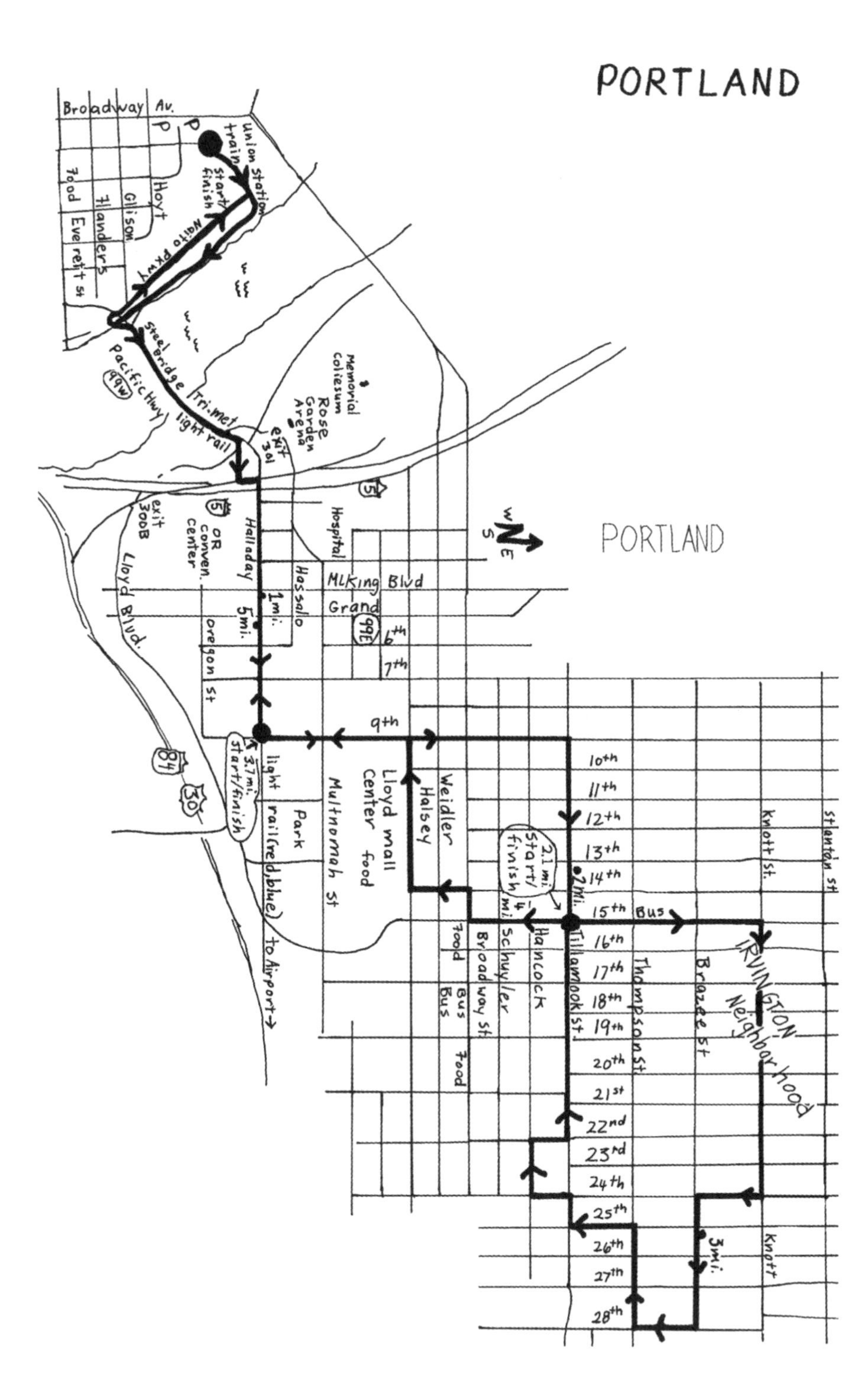
Broadway Av.
Union station
train
start/finish
Hoyt
Glison
Flanders
Everett st
Food
Naito Pkwy
Steel Bridge
Pacific Hwy
99W
Tri-met
light rail
Memorial Coliseum
Rose Garden Arena
exit 301
5
exit 300B
OR conven. center
Hospital
Halladay
Hassalo
MLKing Blvd
Grand
99E
6th
7th
1 mi.
.5 mi.
oregon st
Lloyd Blvd.
84
30
3.7 mi. start/finish
light rail (red, blue) to Airport
Park
Multnomah st
Lloyd mall center food
Halsey
Weidler
9th
10th
11th
12th
13th
14th
15th
16th
17th
18th
19th
20th
21st
22nd
23rd
24th
25th
26th
27th
28th
2.1 mi. start/finish
1/4 mi.
.2 mi.
Bus
Food
Bus
Broadway st
Schuyler
Hancock
Tillamook st.
Thompson st
Brazee st
Knott st.
Stanton st
IRVINGTON Neighborhood
3 mi.
Knott
PORTLAND

PARKS, PSU, POWELL'S

PORTLAND

Distances: 2.8 mi. flat, 4.7 mi. 144 ft. ascent
OR 3.2 mi. At 6th and Yamhill take the FREE Tri-Met back to Union Station.

At Union Station, your back to the frontdoor,
R on to NW Station Way.
L on Marshall St.
L on NW 13th.

Tanner Springs Park

L on NW Everett, 1 block
R on NW 12th, 2 blocks
L on NW Couch, 1 block
R on NW 11th.
·Powell's Books at 10th and Burnside
L on Alder 1 block.
R on 10th, 3 blocks.
L on Taylor 1 block.
R on SW Park. At Salmon St., walk in middle of boulevard.
(2.8 mi, **L** on Salmon. See ✱.

L on College St.
Cross 4th. Jog left, then veer right across plaza, to take steps going down.
L to fountain.
R just past fountain.

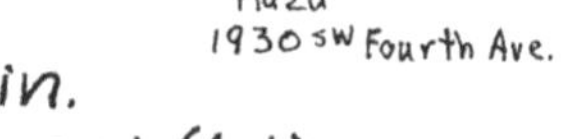

Plaza
1930 SW Fourth Ave.

Down steps, cross street, (1st)
L where steps end. Cross Harrison.
Go **R**. At light, cross Naito Pkwy.
Straight 50 ft. **L** on downhill path.
Straight to river, on Montgomery.
L on river path.

L at ampitheater to Salmon St.
R on 2nd, 2 blocks. ✱
L on Yamhill. (3.2 mi. bus to Union Station)
R on 6th. **R** on Oak, 2 blocks.
L on 4th. **L** on Davis, 2 blocks.
R on 6th to Union Station.

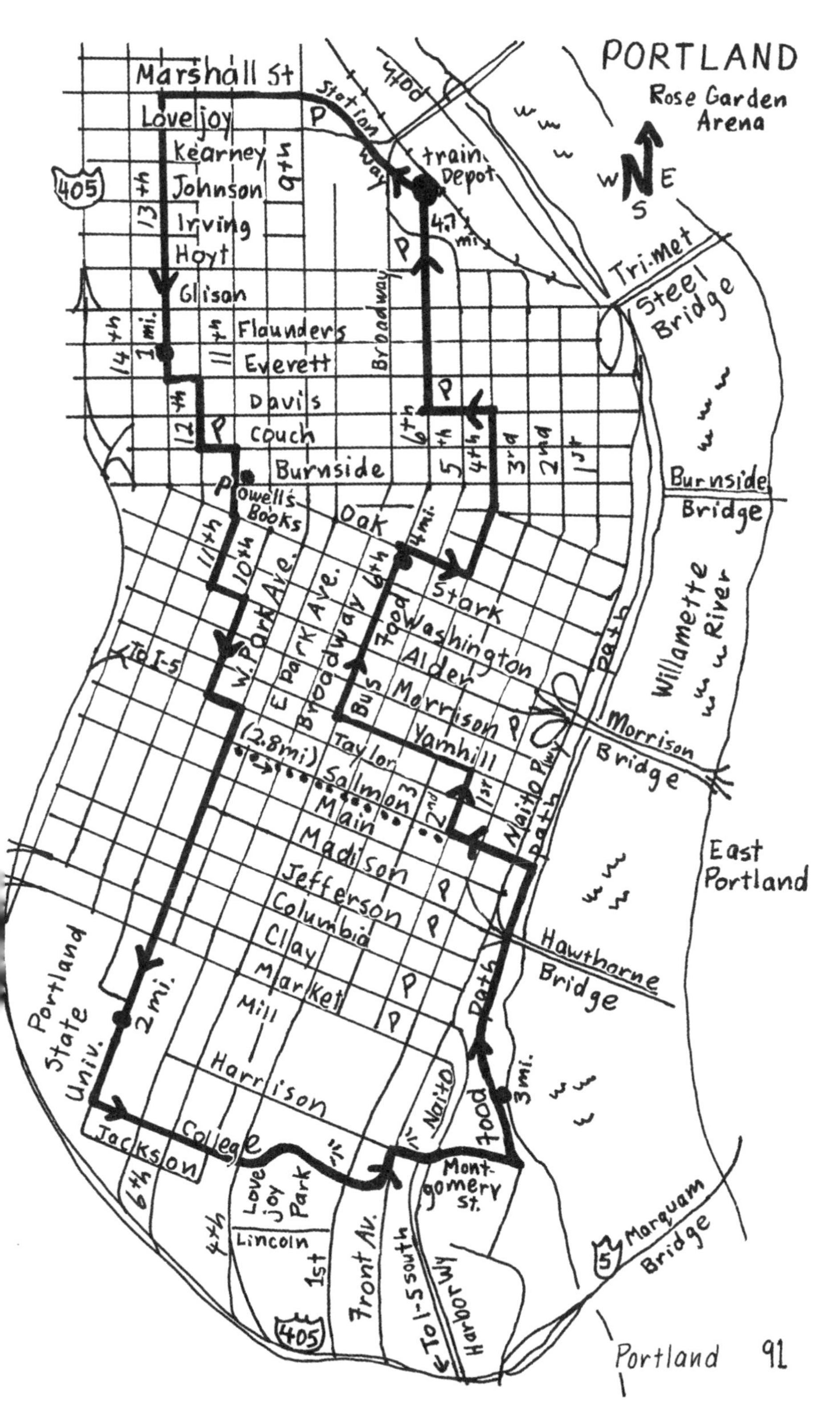

PORTLAND
Rose Garden Arena
N
W
E
S
Marshall St
Lovejoy
Kearney
Johnson
Irving
Hoyt
Glisan
Flaunders
Everett
Davis
Couch
Burnside
Powell's Books
Oak
Stark
Washington
Alder
Morrison
Yamhill
Taylor
Sallmon
Main
Madison
Jefferson
Columbia
Clay
Market
Mill
Harrison
College
Jackson
Lincoln
Montgomery St.
Station Way
train Depot
Tri-Met
Steel Bridge
Burnside Bridge
Morrison Bridge
Hawthorne Bridge
Marquam Bridge
Willamette River
East Portland
Portland State Univ.
Love joy Park
Naito Pkwy
Naito
Path
Bus
Food
Broadway
W. Park Ave.
E Park Ave.
Front Av.
Harbor Wy
To I-5 south
To I-5
405
5
13th
14th
12th
11th
10th
9th
6th
5th
4th
3rd
2nd
1st
1 mi.
2 mi.
(2.8mi)
3 mi.
4 mi.
4.7 mi

PEARL and PIGS on 23rd

PORTLAND

Distances: 1 mi. flat or 2.3 mi. flat
4 mi. 127 ft. ascent or 6 mi. 145 ft. ascent.

Start/finish at Union Station train.
Go up and over the pedestrian bridge.
Straight, down steps, across street (Naito Pkwy).
L on river path (Willamette River)
through iron gate, around building.

R onto path by Albers Mill plaque.
L off path to SW 9th St.
Cross Naito Pkwy.
Walk on right side of SW 9th.
R into pedestrian mall on Kearney St.
(for 1 mi, **L** on Everett, **L** on 6th)
(for 2.3 mi, **L** on Everett. see * below.)

Cobblestones on Kearney St.

L on NW 20th.
R on NW Hoyt St.
R on NW 21st.
L on Marshall St. Cross 22nd. Take path on R side of hospital entrance.
Up stairs. Cross NW 23rd.
R on NW 26th.
R on Vaughan
R on 23rd Place.
L on Thurmon.
R on 23rd.

(for 4 mi. go
L on 23rd
L on Everett
L on 6th

Episcopal Church Door

L on Everett St. *
R on NW 3rd for 2 blocks.
L on Couch for 2 blocks.
(Sat. & Sun. Market under bridge.)
L on Everett for 2 blocks.
R on 3rd one block.
L on Flaunders for 3 blocks.
R on 6th to train station.

Chinese Gardens
3rd and Everett

PORTLAND

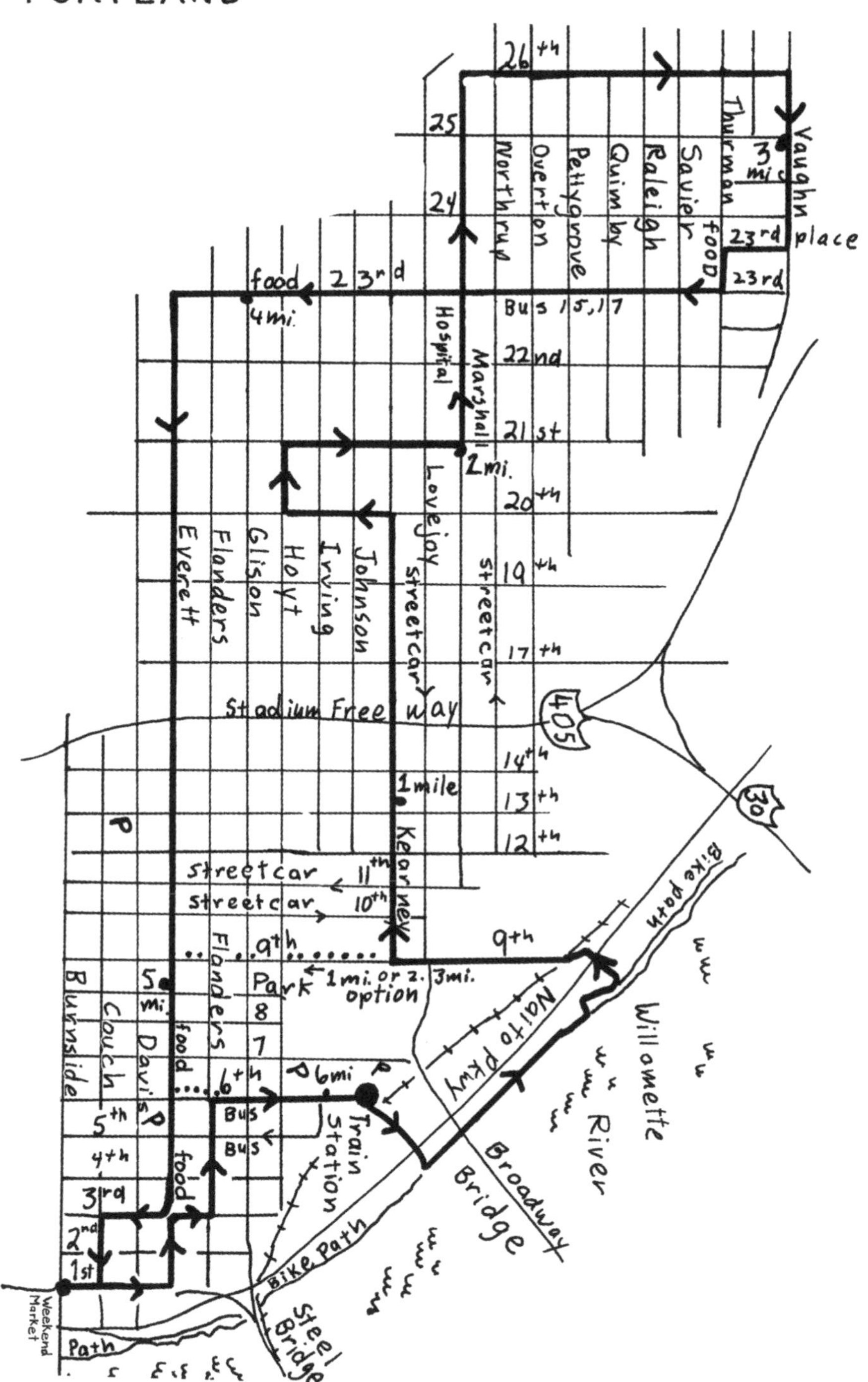

26th
25
24
Northrup
Overton
Pettygrove
Quimby
Raleigh
Savier
Thurman
Vaughn
3 mi
FOOD
23rd place
23rd
food
4mi.
23rd
Bus 15,17
Hospital
Marshall
22nd
21st
2mi.
20th
Lovejoy
19th
Everett
Flanders
Glison
Hoyt
Irving
Johnson
streetcar
streetcar
17th
Stadium Freeway
405
14th
1mile
13th
Kearney
12th
30
streetcar
11th
streetcar
10th
Bike path
9th
9th
Flanders
Park
1mi. or 2. option
3mi.
Naito Pkwy
Burnside
5
5 mi.
Couch
Davis
food
8
7
Willamette
River
6th
6mi
Train Station
5th
Bus
Bus
4th
food
3rd
Broadway
Bridge
2nd
1st
Bike Path
Weekend Market
Path
Steel Bridge

RIVER LOOP to OMSI

Oregon Museum of Science & Industry

PORTLAND

Distances: 2mi., 2.85mi. or 4.3mi. Flat.

Start/finish at Union Station train depot. 800NW 6th.
With your back to the front entrance,
L to the corner.
L to steps. Go up.
Straight to river. **R** on river path.
L across railroad tracks.
L at 2 big steel sculptures. Over bridge.

R at end of bridge on river path.
(for **2mi.** return over Burnside Bridge)
(for 2.85 mi. return over Morrison Bridge)
see * below for directions to finish.

At OMSI continue to end, Return to Hawthorne
Return to Hawthorne Bridge.
Cross bridge. **R** down steps.(toilet)
L along river path.

* At the 2 big steel sculptures,
continue, cross railroad track.
L after tracks.
R along street. (Naito).
L at big pedistrian crossing.
Up steps to bridge.
Cross bridge to Union Station.

OR Convention center

walk to OMSI 40min.

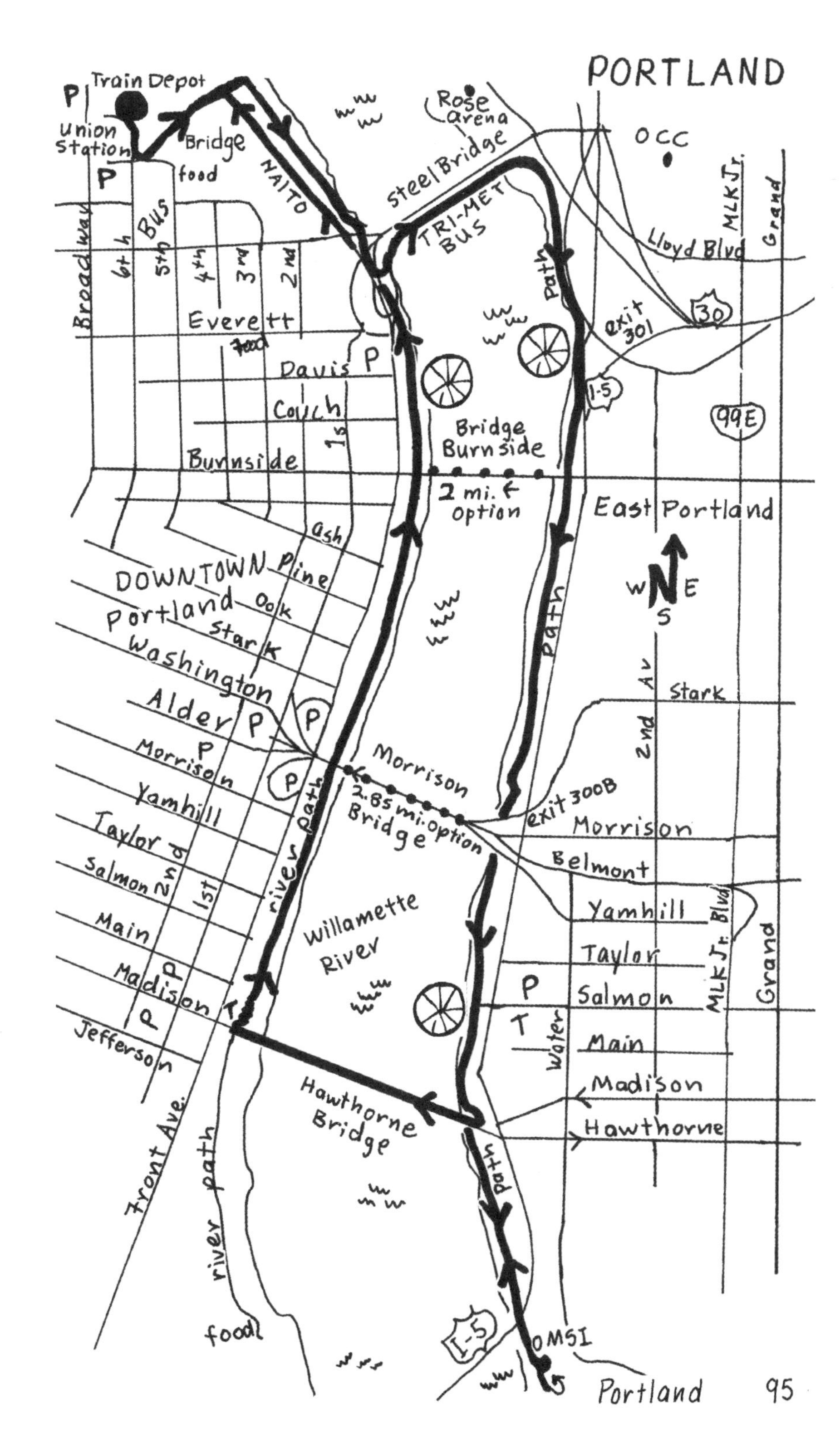
PORTLAND
Train Depot
Union Station
Bridge
food
NAITO
Rose arena
Steel Bridge
TRI-MET BUS
OCC
MLK Jr.
Grand
Lloyd Blvd
Path
exit 301
30
I-5
99E
Broadway
6th
5th
Bus
4th
3rd
2nd
Everett
Davis
Couch
1st
Bridge Burnside
Burnside
2 mi. option
East Portland
Ash
DOWNTOWN
Pine
Portland
Oak
Stark
Washington
Alder
Morrison
Yamhill
Taylor
Salmon
2nd
Main
Madison
Jefferson
1st
river path
Morrison
2.85 mi. option
Bridge
exit 300B
2nd Av
Stark
Morrison
Belmont
Yamhill
MLK Jr. Blvd
Willamette River
Taylor
Salmon
Main
Madison
Hawthorne
Water
Hawthorne Bridge
Front Ave.
river path
food
OMSI
I-5
W
N
E
S

LADD ADD. to RIVER

from I-5, north: Exit 300B toward Oregon City.
R on 11th. L on Hawthorne.
from I-5, South: Exit 300 for I-84. R toward Yamhill.
R on Water. R on Hawthorne.
L at Madison. Sharp L at Hawthorne

Distances: 2.3 mi. flat, through Ladd circle area.
3.7 mi. flat. 20th Ave. to River. See * below.
6 mi. Combine both walks.

Start/finish at Hawthorne and 20th Ave.
Walk down diagonal Elliot Street, on right of 1960 store.
L at end, Ladd circle, at corner,
L on Harrison, 1 block. R on Cypress.
L on 20th. R on Division.

SE 20 + Hawthorne

R on Tamarak.
L on Orange.
R on Division. R on 12th
R on Spruce.
R on Harrison. L at end.
L on corner to Ladd.

2456 SE Tamarack
Mizpah Presbyterian church
1891

R on Hawthorne. R on Maple
L on Poplar. R on Hawthorne.
End of 2.3 mi. walk.

2243 Cypress resident hens

*At Hawthorne and 20th L, or north, cross Hawthorne.
L on Madison. R on 13th 1 block.
L on Main. L on Grand 1 block.
R on Madison, over river.
R down first steps (restroom)

L on river path. At river post #287,
L to Morrison. Hotel 50 is on left.
Up ramp on right side.
After river, R down steps.
L on river path.

L on Salmon St. under I-5 (restrooms).
R on 20th to finish.

Portland

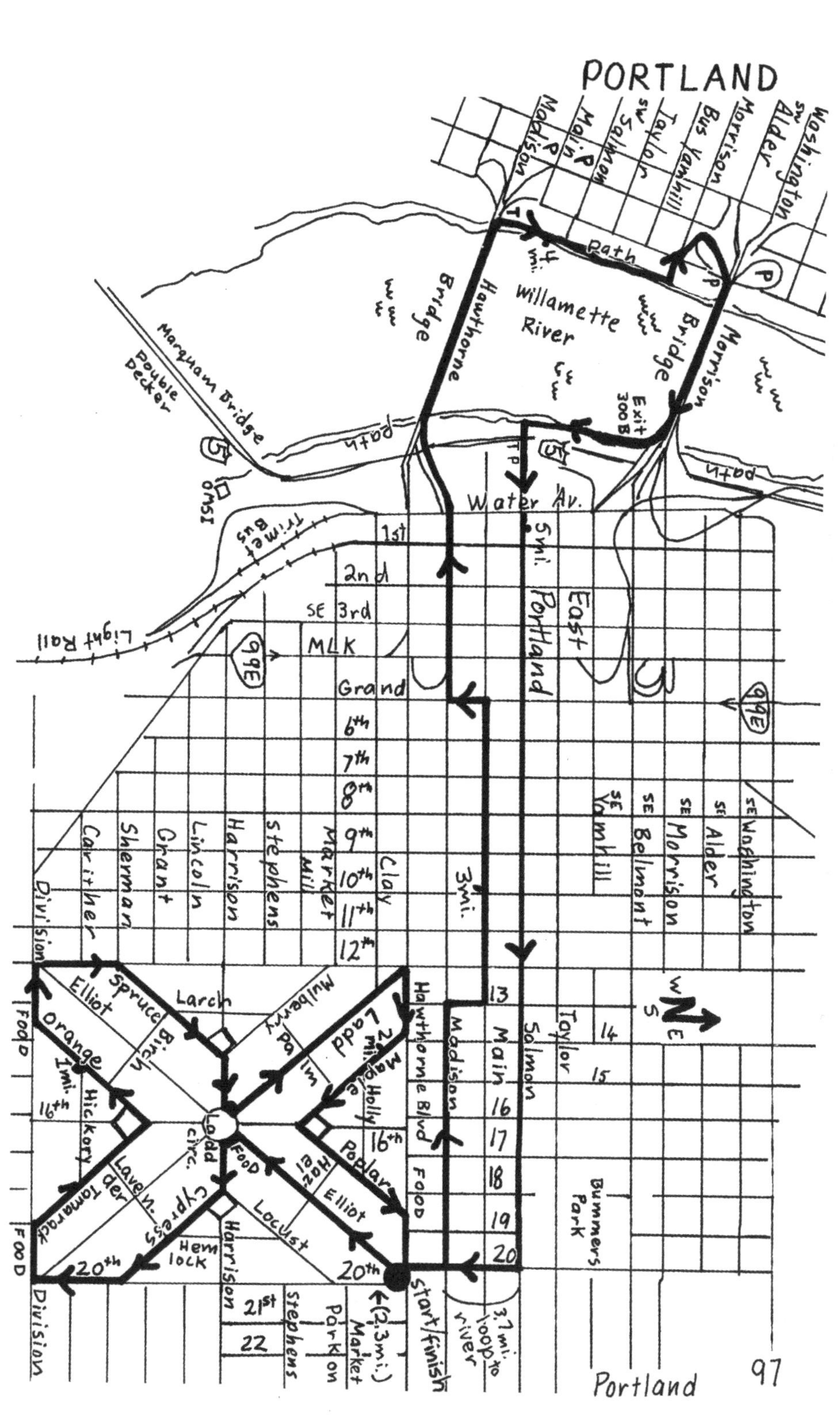

PORTLAND
Madison
Main
SW Salmon
Taylor
Bus Yamhill
Morrison
SW Alder
Washington
Path
.4 mi.
Hawthorne Bridge
Willamette River
Morrison Bridge
Exit 300B
Marquam Bridge
Double Decker
path
I 5
OMSI
TP
Water Av.
1st
2nd
SE 3rd
MLK
Grand
6th
7th
8th
9th
10th
11th
12th
99E
Light Rail
Trimet Bus
5 mi.
Portland
East
3 mi.
Clay
Market
Mill
Stephens
Harrison
Lincoln
Grant
Sherman
Caruther
Division
SE Yamhill
SE Belmont
SE Morrison
SE Alder
SE Washington
13
14
15
16
17
18
19
20
Hawthorne Blvd
Madison
Main
Salmon
Taylor
N
W
E
S
Larch
Spruce
Elliot
Orange
Birch
Mulberry
Palm
Ladd
2 mi.
Maple
Holly
1 mi.
16th
Hickory
Ladd circ.
Lavender
Tamarack
Laven.
Cypress
FOOD
Hazel
Elliot
Poplar
Locust
Harrison
Hemlock
20th
21st
22
Stephens
Park
Market
(2.3 mi.)
Start/finish
3.7 mi. loop to river
Bummers Park

TRAM and TROLLEY

PORTLAND

Distances: 2.5 mi. 152 ft. elevation. 4 mi. 468 ft. elevation. 4.6 and 7 mi. 611 ft. elevation gain.

Start/finish at Union station. 800 NW 6th.
With your back to the front entrance,
Veer **L**, on 6th st. **R** on Flaunders.
R on 15th, 1 block. Cross Glisan.
L across 15th. Cross bridge. Cross 16th.
L on 16th, 1 block. **R** on Flaunders.

1832 SW Elm St.

view to downtown from Vista View Viaduct Bridge

L on 21st. **R** on Salmon.
L on King Ave.
R on Main.
L on 22nd.
R on King Court. **L** on Vista Ave.

(for 2.5 mi, **L** on Salmon. On 10th, catch streetcar. See * below.)

After big curve, sharp **R** on sw Montgomery.
L on Elm. **R** on 18th. **R** on Elizabeth, curve left.
Straight to Terrace. **R** on Gerald. Down Stairs.

(for 4 mi. **L** on Clifton. follow map.)

Cross street (Broadway Av.)
Look left for trail sign. follow trail to Marquam Shelter.
Opposite the shelter, on **R** follow trail up .6 mi. to OHSU. **L** on Connor Trail,

On top, veer **L** through parking lot.
L on Street (Kohler), to Admin. Campus.
Cross the bridge on your right.
L down stairs, down hill on sidewalk.
R in P. Kohler Pavilion to Tram.
(restrooms on **L** before tram.)

Tram is free on ride down
open M-F 6-10, Sa. 9-5

Exit tram. **R** along trolley tracks. Cross street to board
(7 mi. follow trolley tracks to Glisan.) Free ride to Glisan.
(4.6 mi. take trolley to Glisan.)
At Glisan, walk downhill to 6th. *
L on 6th to Union Station finish.

marigold pot

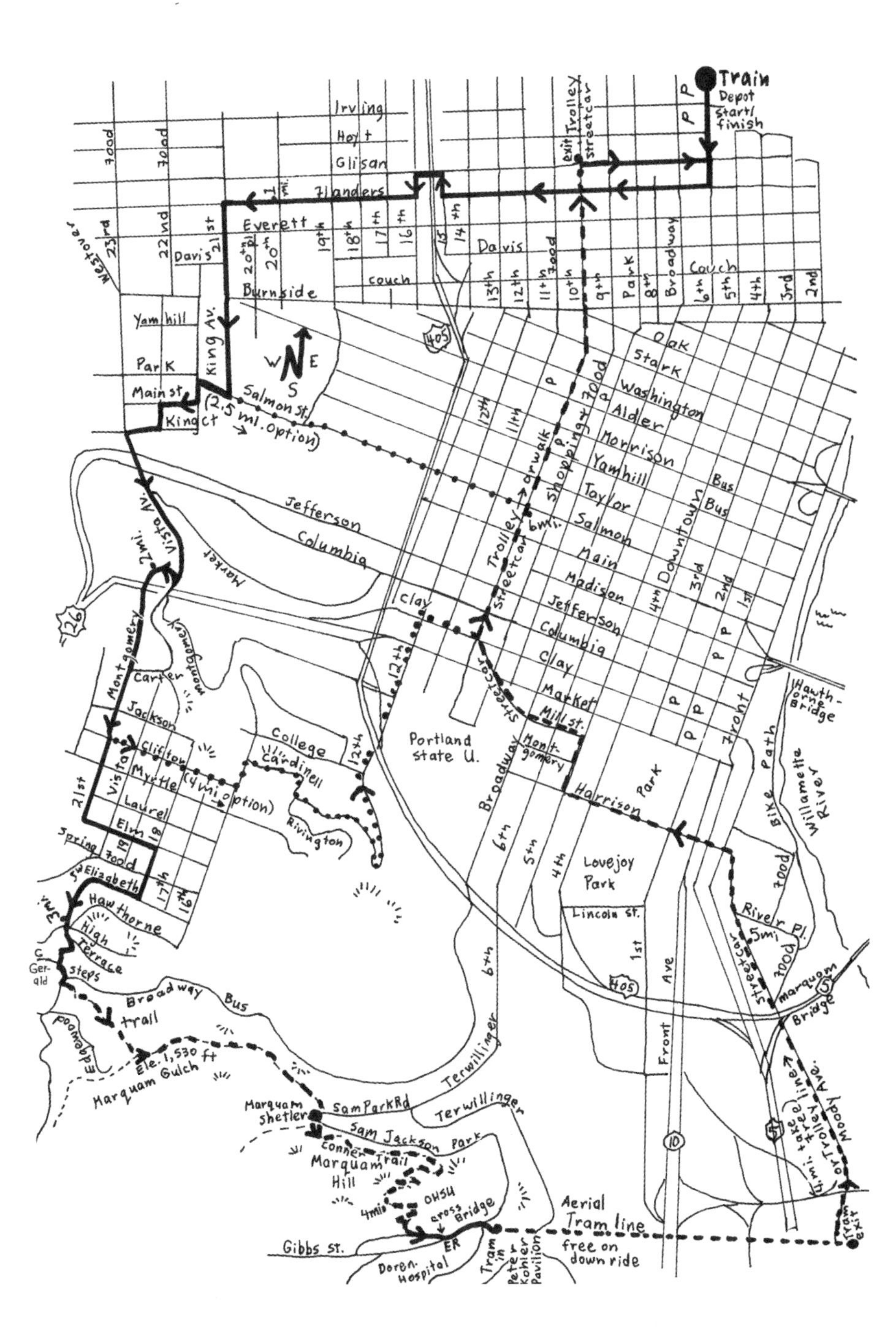

Train
Depot
Start/
finish
exit Trolley streetcar
Irving
Hoyt
Glisan
Flanders
Everett
Davis
Couch
Burnside
1 mi.
Westover
23rd
22nd
21st
20th Pl
20th
19th
18th
17th
16th
15
14th
13th
12th
11th
10th
9th
Park
8th
Broadway
6th
5th
4th
3rd
2nd
Yamhill
Park
Main st
King Ct
King Av.
Salmon st.
(2.5 mi. option)
Oak
Stark
Washington
Alder
Morrison
Yamhill
Taylor
Salmon
Main
Madison
Jefferson
Columbia
Clay
Market
Mill st.
Bus
Downtown
Shopping
Trolley streetcar
Trolley or walk
6 mi.
Jefferson
Columbia
Market
Vista Av.
2 mi.
Montgomery
Carter
Jackson
Clifton
Myrtle
Laurel
Elm
Spring
SW Elizabeth
Hawthorne
High
Terrace
steps
Gerald
3 mi.
21st
Vista
19
18
17th
16th
(4 mi. option)
College
Cardinell
Rivington
12th
Portland State U.
Broadway
Mont-gomery
Harrison
Park
6th
5th
4th
Lovejoy Park
Lincoln St.
1st
Ave
Front
Front
Streetcar
Hawthorne Bridge
Willamette River
Bike Path
River Pl.
5 mi.
Marquam Bridge
Broadway Bus
trail
Edgewood
Ele. 1,530 ft
Marquam Gulch
Terwilliger
Marquam shelter
Sam Park Rd
Sam Jackson Park
Conner Trail
Marquam Hill
4 mi.
OHSU
cross Bridge
ER
Gibbs st.
Doren. Hospital
Tram in
Peter Kohler Pavilion
Aerial Tram line
free on down ride
4 mi. take tree line or Trolley
Moody Ave.
Tram exit

ROGUE RIVER

City, State Park and Rest Area

Distance: 2 mi. in City of Rogue River. Flat.
3 mile riverside path connects the city, state park and rest area.

From I-5: exit 48, toward city of Rogue River.
Take Depot St. to Main St., 1 block.
R on Gardiner into free parking lot and restrooms.

Skevington Crossing

OR start at either the Rest Area or Valley of Rogue Rv. State Park.

R on E. Main. **L** on Cedar
Cross Third St, go **L**.
Cross Oak, go **R** for 1/2 block.
L on Third, 1 block.
L on Pine to cross walk light.
Cross Pine at light, go **R**.

L into Rogue R.C. Church lot.
Continue to path, across bridge.
L after bridge to circle the park. Note list of trees on a sign by the parking lot.
Return over bridge to Pine St.

R on Pine, 1 block. **R** on Fourth.
L on Berglund. **L** on Main.
R on Depot St. to river.

① **R** to Greenway Path to Valley of Roq. Rr. St. Park or rest area. It is 3 miles from bridge to the Rest Area. Do some!
② Walk to middle of bridge and return on Depot St.

R on Main to parking lot at Gardiner.

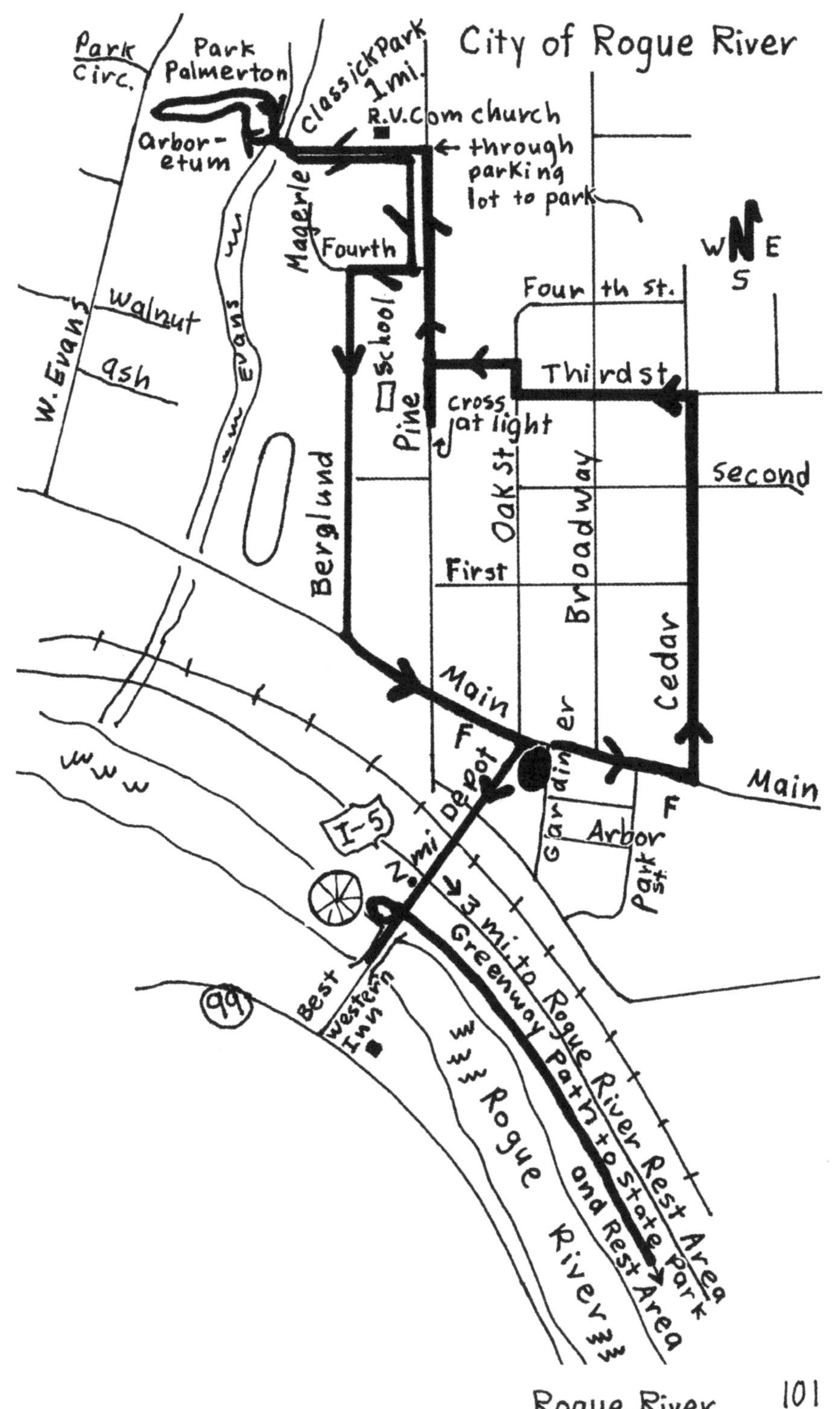
City of Rogue River
Park Circ.
Park Palmerton
Classick Park 1mi.
R.V.Com church
through parking lot to park
Arbor-etum
Magerle
Fourth
W
N
E
S
Fourth st.
Walnut
W. Evans
Evans
ash
school
Third st
Pine
cross at light
Second
Berglund
Oak st
Broadway
First
Cedar
Main
F
Gardiner
Depot
Main
F
I-5
Arbor
Park st
½ mi
3 mi. to Rogue River Rest Area
Greenway Path to State Park and Rest Area
Best Western Inn
99
Rogue River

AROUND DOWTOWN

Roseburg

Distance: 3mi. or 4 mi.

start/finish: Visitor Center at Spruce and Douglas

gazebo

From I-5, exit 124 to OR-138 to City Center. Merge on Harvard/138. Continue on 138 over bridge. Just after bridge, **L** on Spruce. Park at Visitor Center.

With your back to the Visitor Center entrance, **L** to path. **L** on path, under building. Stay on path along river, under 2 bridges. You emerge on Flint st.

R on Lane, 1 block. **L** on Fullerton, 1 blk.
L on Mosher. **R** on Pine.
R on Rice, 1 block. **R** on Mill st.
At end, jog **L** then **R** on Sheridan.
R on Cass, 1 block.
L on Pine, 1 block. **R** on Oak.
R on Rose. **L** on Lane, 1 block.
R on Jackson. Jogs at Mosher.
L on Roberts, 1 block.
L on Hamilton. **R** on Orcutt Av.

on mosher

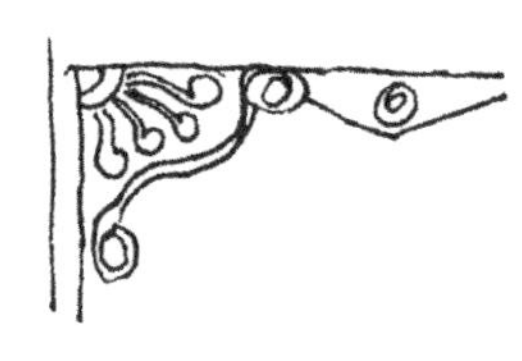

L on Main st., 1 block.
R up Hawthorne, 1 block.
L on Kane.
L on Lane, 2 blocks.

R on Jackson. **R** on Washington.
L on Kane, 1 block.
L on Douglas to end.

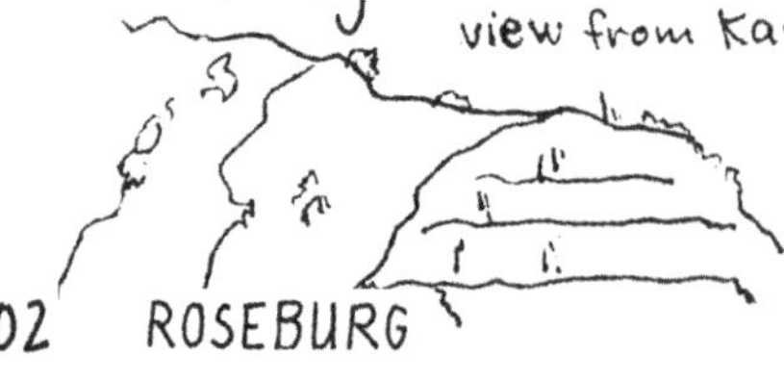

view from Kane st.

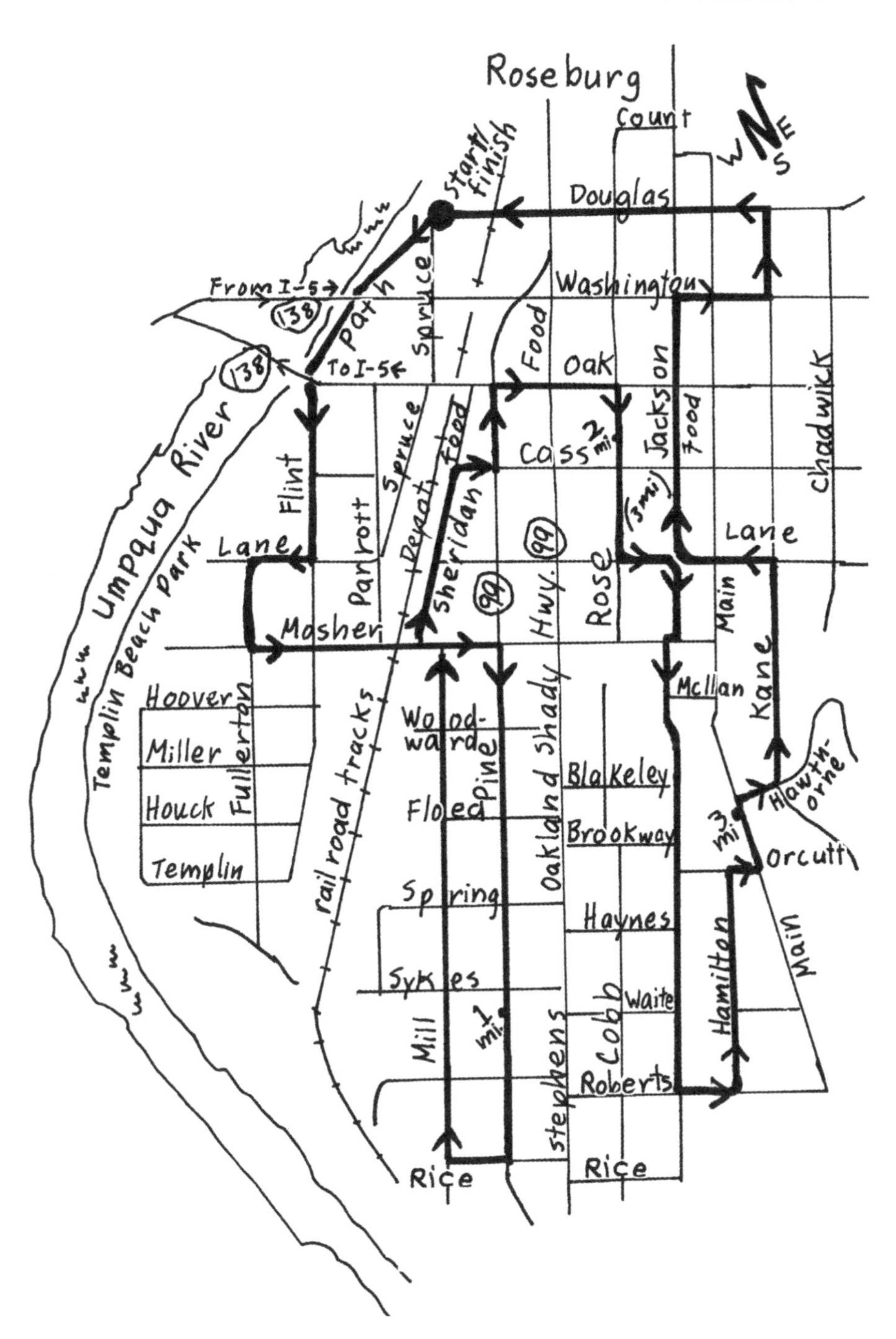
Roseburg
start/finish
Douglas
Washington
Oak
Cass
Lane
Mosher
Flint
Parrott
Spruce
Depot
Sheridan
Food
Hwy. 99
Rose
Jackson
Main
Kane
Chadwick
Umpqua River
Templin Beach Park
From I-5
To I-5
138
Path
Hoover
Miller
Houck
Templin
Fullerton
railroad tracks
Woodward
Floed
Spring
Sykes
Mill
Pine
Oakland Shady
Stephens
Blakeley
Brookway
Haynes
Waite
Cobb
Roberts
Rice
McIlan
Hawthorne
Orcutt
Hamilton
1 mi.
2 mi.
3 mi.
(3 mi)
N
S
E
W

LAUREWOOD PARK, RIVER

Roseburg

Distance: 2.8 miles. Flat.

Start/finish: Visitor Center at Spruce and Douglas.

From I-5, exit 124 to OR-138 to City Center. Merge on Harvard/138. Continue on 138 over bridge. **L** on Spruce, just after bridge. Park at Visitor Center.

With your back to the Visitor Center entrance,
L to path. **L** on path, under building.
L through garden to street.
R on street, (Spruce).
R on Washington, over river.

R on Madrone.
R on Lilburn.
L on Riverside.
L on Casey.
L on Chapman.
R on Madrone.

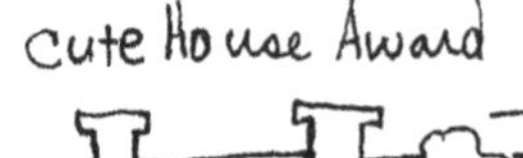

R on Harvard. At next street, jog **R** then **L** to bike path.
R on foot bridge over river.
R on path, curves right, following the river.
Path becomes SE Pine St.
R on SE Douglas to finish.

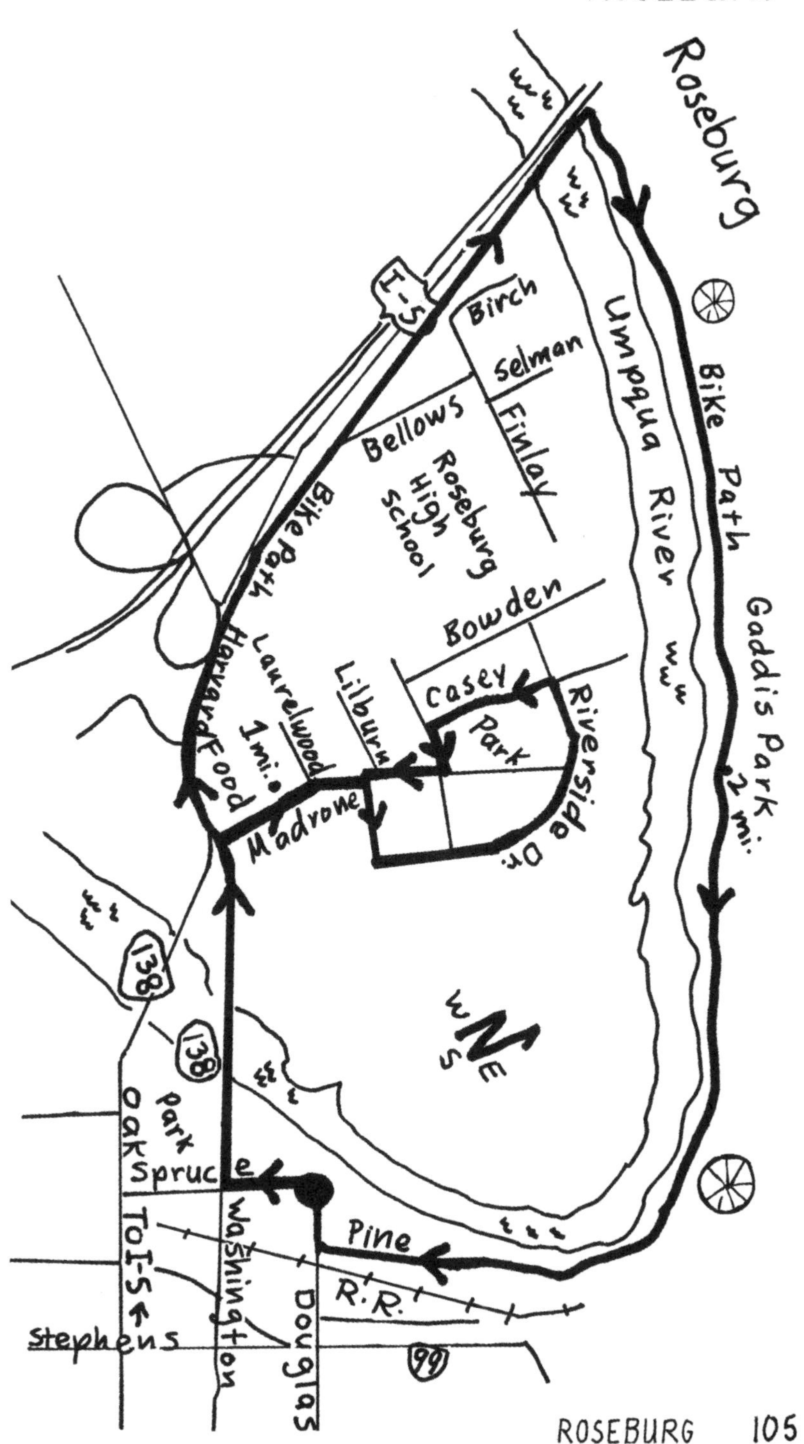
Roseburg
I-5
Birch
Selman
Finlay
Umpqua River
Bike Path
Gaddis Park
2 mi.
Bellows
Roseburg High School
Bike Path
Bowden
Casey
Park
Riverside Dr.
Lilburn
Laurelwood
1 mi.
Harvard
Food
Madrone
138
138
Park
Oak
Spruce
Washington
Douglas
Pine
R.R.
To I-5
Stephens
99
N
E
S
W

VETERANS and RIVER

Roseburg

Distance: 2.7mi. or 4.5 miles. Flat.

Start/finish: Stewart Park at Garden Valley/Goetz.
From I-5, exit 125 for Garden Valley, to Roseburg.
Follow signs to Veterans Hospt. Pass it and
Fred Meyer. **L** on Goetz to Stewart Park lot.

VA Hospital
Thank you to our Veterans!

Walk back to Garden Valley, go **R.**
R into Veterans, on sidewalk
along chain link fence.
Cross first street to stay on
sidewalk.
At "Parking Lot B" sign, **R** 20 paces.
L on to sidewalk, through walkway
and parking lot.
R at street, Estelle, curves to
south exit.

(For 2.7 mi. option, **R** after exit, see ✱ below.)

L after exit, through disc course.
R at fork in path, downhill.
R across river on footbridge.
R after bridge to street (Esperanza).
L on Umpqua. Cross Harvard.
R on Military Road. **R** on Myrtle, 1 block.
R on Wharton. Cross Harvard, go **L.**
R on Cemetery Rd, straight to
path, curves **R** along river.

South Umpqua River

L over bridge. **L** before Veteran's gate.
✱ Stay on path, pass train engine.
R on path along chain link fence.

Through golf course parking lot,
Path curves **R** around golf
driving range.
Pass the pond on your left,
back to Stewart Park.

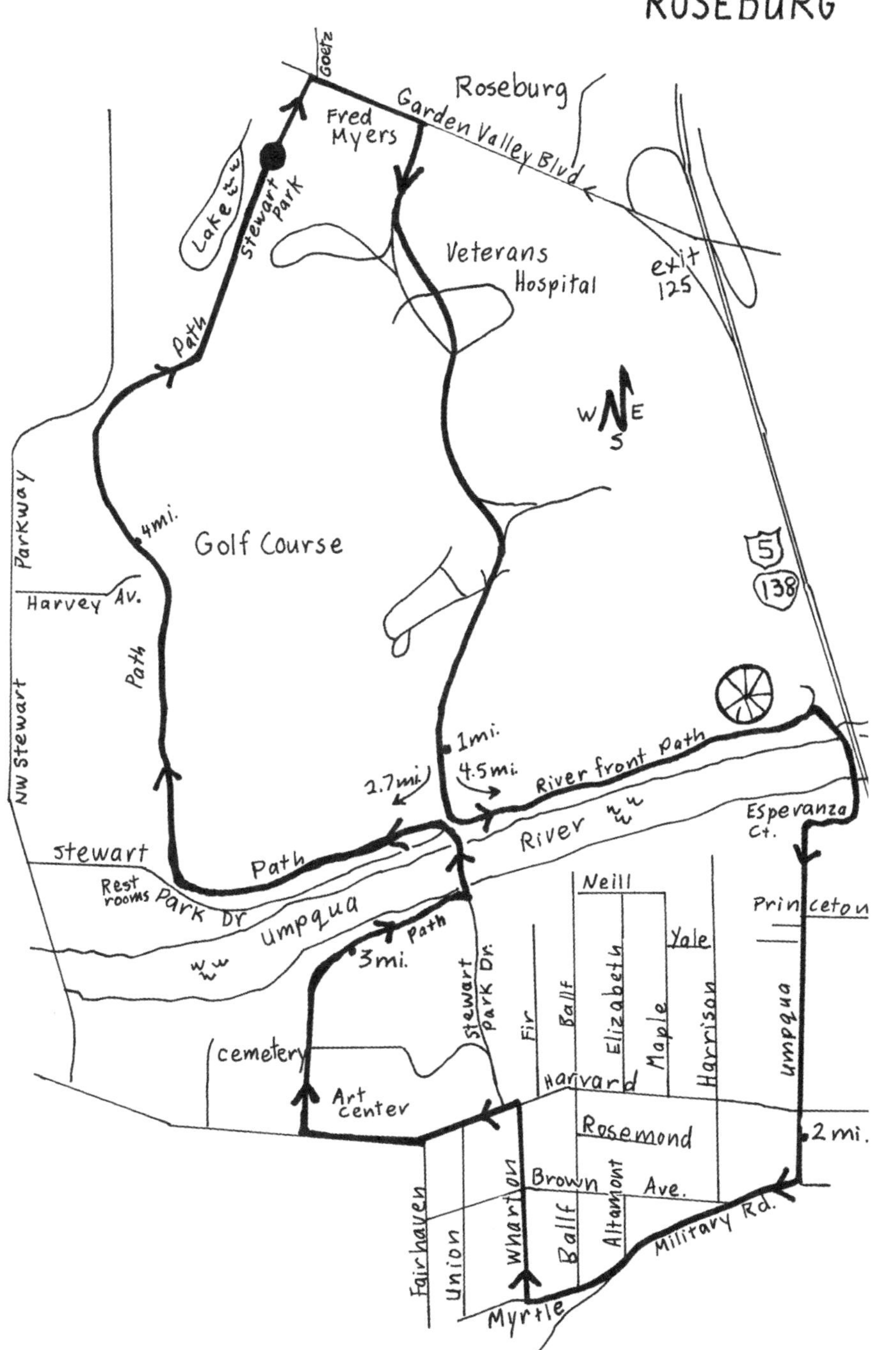
Goetz
Roseburg
Garden Valley Blvd
Fred Myers
Lake
Stewart park
Veterans Hospital
exit 125
Path
W N E S
4mi.
Golf Course
Parkway
Harvey Av.
Path
5
138
NW Stewart
1mi.
4.5mi.
2.7mi.
River front Path
River
Esperanza Ct.
Stewart
Path
Rest rooms
Park Dr
Umpqua
Neill
Princeton
Path
3mi.
Yale
Stewart Park Dr.
Fir
Ballf
Elizabeth
Maple
Harrison
Umpqua
cemetery
Harvard
Art center
Rosemond
2mi.
Brown Ave.
Fairhaven
Union
Wharton
Ballf
Altamont
Military Rd.
Myrtle

SALEM Directions, Lodging

All walks begin at the Mission Mill, also the Visitor Center, at 12th and Mill. Open M-Sa. 10-5
The Amtrak depot is one block away.
With your back to the depot, R on 12th. R on Mill.

Directions from I-5 to Mission Mill, visitor center:
Exit 253, to city center on Mission/ Hwy 22, toward visitor center. R on 13th 1 block. R on Mill.

Nearby lodging; distance from depot. Ask for a ride.

1. Phoenix Inn, Convention Center. (.7mi.) 201 Liberty, 1-877-540-7800
2. Travelodge. 17th and State St. (.4mi.) 1-800-578-7878
3. Bookmark B+B. (1mi.) 975 D st. NE 1-503-399-2013
4. Betty's B+B (1mi.) 965 D st. NE 1-503-399-7848.
5. Cottonwood Cottage B+B (1mi.) 960 E st. NE 1-800-349-3979.
6. Creekside Garden B+B, (.8 mi.) 333 Wyatt Ct 1-503-391-0837
7. City Center Motel (.7mi.) 1-503-364-0121 710 Liberty. Cheap, but dirty, worn.

Stop at the Mission Mill for historical information, a tour, restroom, food.
More history is online at www.travelsalem.com

Thomas Kay Woolen Mill

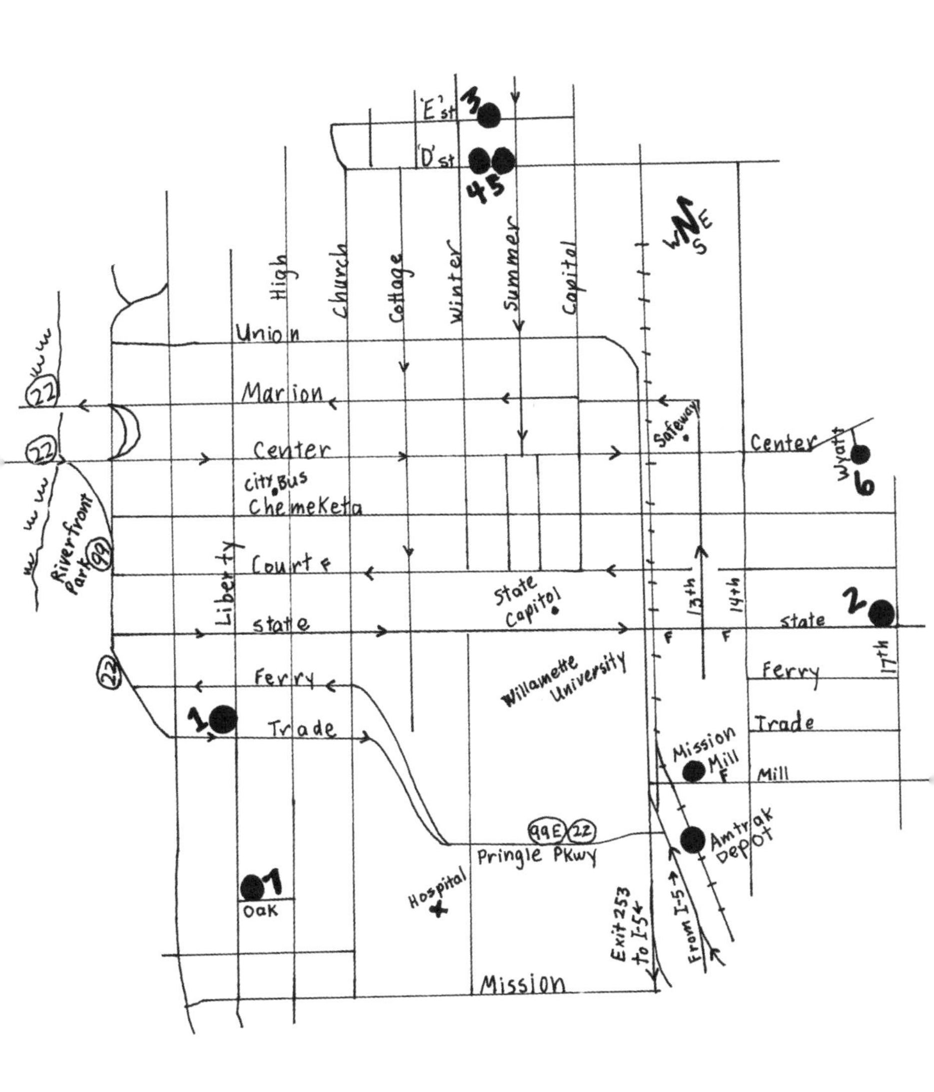
'E' st
3
'D' st
4 5
N
W
E
S
High
Church
Cottage
Winter
Summer
Capitol
Union
Marion
Center
City Bus
Chemeketa
Court
Liberty
State
Ferry
Trade
22
99
Riverfront Park
State Capitol
Willamette University
Safeway
13th
14th
Center
Wyatt
6
2
State
17th
Ferry
Trade
Mill
Mission Mill
Amtrak Depot
1
99E
22
Pringle Pkwy
Hospital
7
Oak
Exit 253 to I-5
From I-5
Mission

TASTE OF SALEM

Distance: 3.5 or 5.1 miles. Flat.

Start/finish: Mission Mill, 12th and Mill.
L on 12th, 1 block.
R on Pringle Parkway. First **R** into parking lot, curves left.
R at eagle nest statue.
Straight across plaza.
over bridge.
R on path between Eaton Hall and Smullin Hall to street.
R on sidewalk to 12th
L on 12th, 1/2 block. **L** into and through parking lot. Pass the circuit rider.

on old post office
12th and State

R around to front of Capitol. With your back to the Capitol, walk straight down the right side.
Jog Left at center. Stay on Summer.
(for 3.5mi. option, **L** on Court.
See * below.

old columns from former capitol

L on D st. 1 block. **L** on Winter St.
R on Court. **L** on Center
* **L** on Liberty.
R on State to Carousel. Ride it!
Restrooms in park. Stroll park path.

Return on State St. **R** on Commercial.
Cross bridge. **L** on path around pond.
Under Liberty, then High St. bridge.
You emerge on Church St. Cross, go **R**.

L into driveway for OR sch. Blind.
veer right through lot. **L** at blue doors.
L at Irvine Hall into Senses Garden.
Explore garden, return. **L** on Church. Cross Mission.
L on Mission. Cross 12th on bridge. **L** at fork.

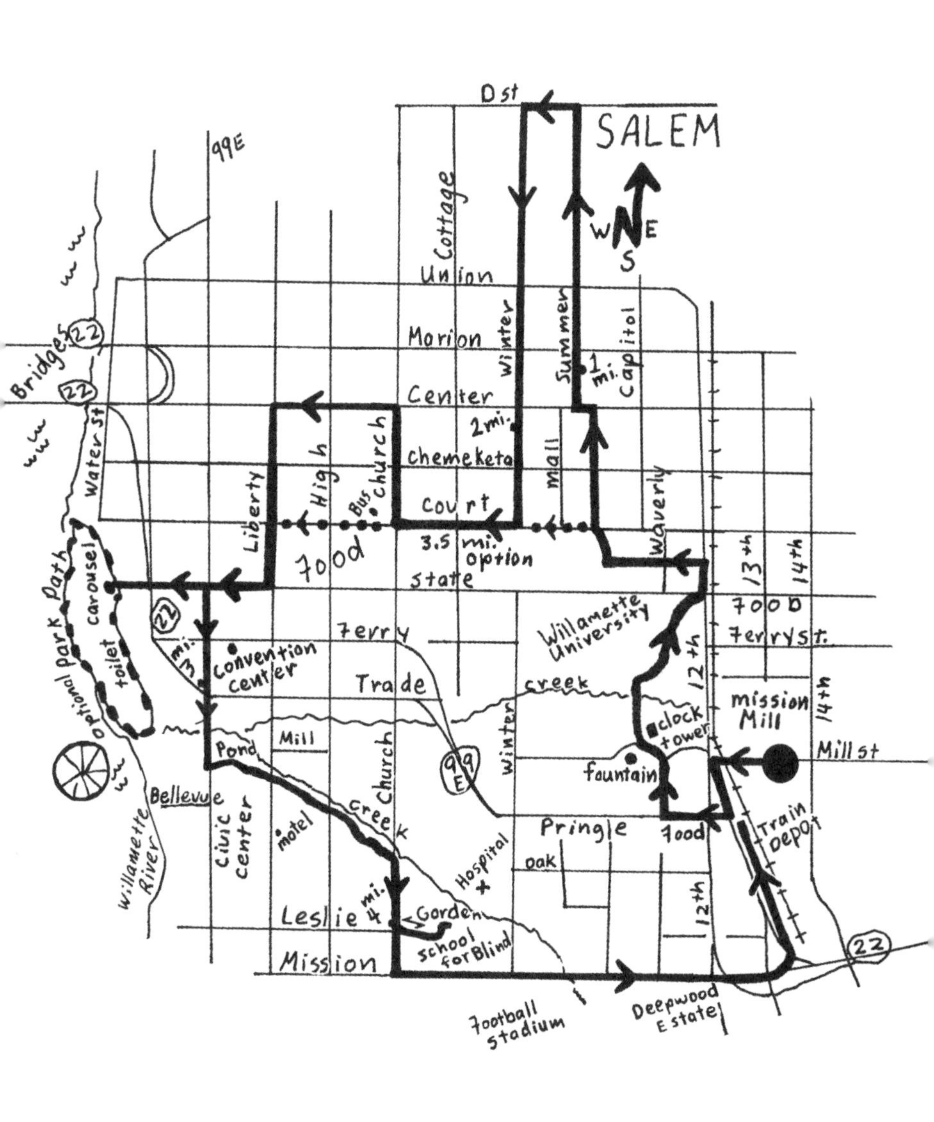
SALEM
D st
99E
Cottage
Union
Marion
Center
Chemeketa
Court
State
Winter
Summer
Capitol
1 mi.
2mi.
Mall
Bridges
22
Water St
Liberty
High
Bus
Church
food
3.5 mi. option
Waverly
13th
14th
Willamette University
Ferry
Ferry st.
Trade
creek
12th
Mission Mill
Mill st
clock tower
fountain
Train Depot
Pringle
Oak
Hospital
Convention center
3 mi.
Mill
Pond
Bellevue
Civic center
motel
Leslie
4 mi.
Garden
School for Blind
Mission
Football Stadium
Deepwood Estate
optional park path
carousel
toilet
Willamette River
99 E

MILL to MANSION

Salem

Distance: 3.5 mi. or 5.1 mi. Elevation: 182 ft.

Start/finish: Mission Mill, 12th and Mill. near train depot
From Mission Mill parking lot,
R on Mill. **L** on 12th.
Pass train depot. **L** on sidewalk under bridge. **R** to 12th.
Cross 12th to Mission.

(for 3.5 mi. option, continue on Mission. **L** on High. see * below.

R on University.
L on Oak, through hospital.
Cross Winter St. go **R**, look left for path along creek just after parking lot. **L** on path. Up steps. **R** on sidewalk. Cross at first crosswalk. Continue **R**, 1 block.

L on path along creek. **R** on High.
L on Court. **L** on Liberty. Cross Trade.
L through water gardens to Street, (High). **R** on High. *
- 883 High. home of Governor, then Senator Mark Hatfield.
- 1043 High, Senator Ben Harding home.

R on Meyers. **L** on Saginaw. **R** on Lincoln.
L on John. **L** on Superior. **R** on Fir.
L on Rural. **L** on High.

Governor's home-State seal on gate

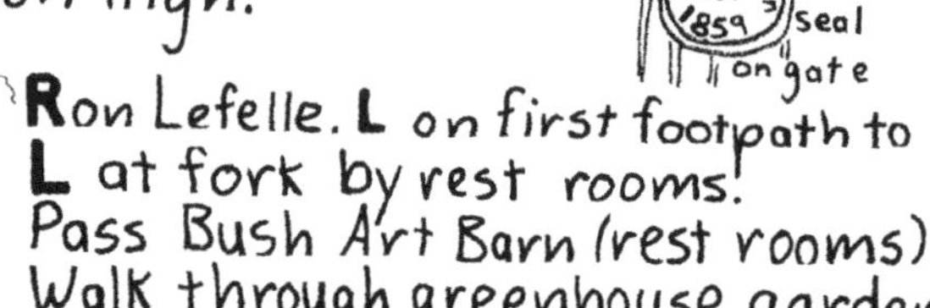

R on Lefelle. **L** on first footpath to **L** at fork by rest rooms.
Pass Bush Art Barn (rest rooms)
Walk through greenhouse, gardens.
In front of Bush home, take downhill sidewalk. **R** on street, Mission.
Cross 12th on bridge.
L at fork under bridge to return.

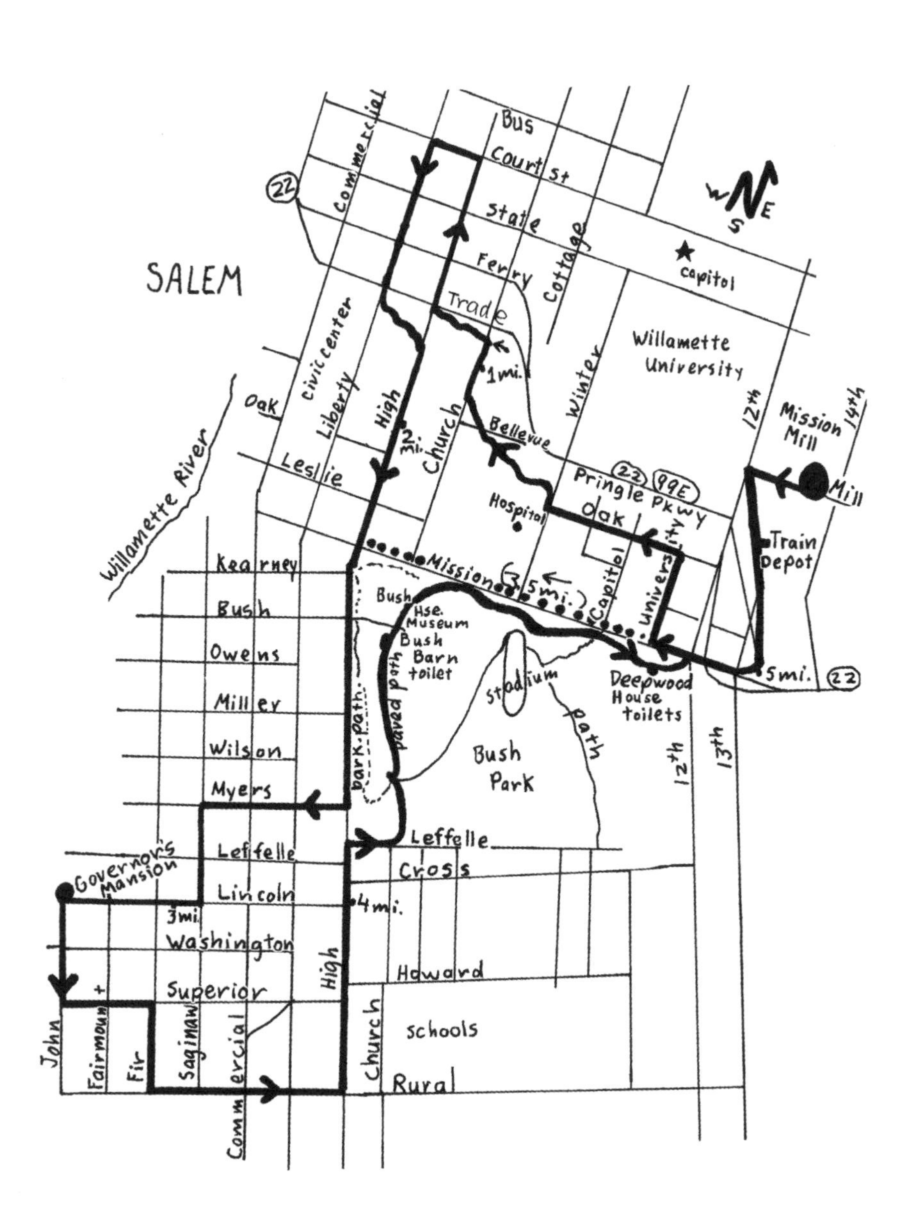
SALEM
Willamette River
Commercial
Bus
Court St
State
Ferry
Trade
Cottage
capitol
Willamette University
Mission Mill
Mill
12th
14th
Winter
Church
High
Liberty
civic center
Oak
Leslie
1mi.
2mi.
Bellevue
Pringle Pkwy
22
99E
Oak
Hospital
University
Capitol
Train Depot
Mission
3.5mi.
Bush
Hse. Museum
Bush Barn toilet
paved path
bark path
stadium
path
Bush Park
Deepwood House toilets
5mi.
12th
13th
Kearney
Bush
Owens
Miller
Wilson
Myers
Leffelle
Lincoln
Governor's Mansion
3mi.
Washington
Superior
Leffelle
Cross
4mi.
Howard
Schools
Rural
John
Fairmount
Fir
Saginaw
Commercial

CAPITOL and CREEKS

Salem

Distance: 3 mi. or 5 mi. Flat.

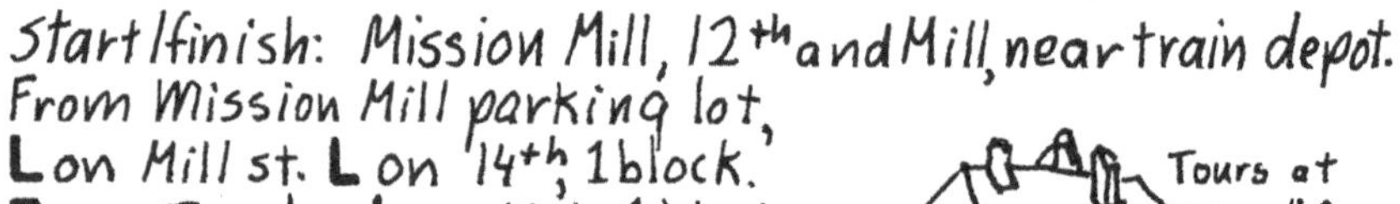

Start/finish: Mission Mill, 12th and Mill, near train depot.
From Mission Mill parking lot,
L on Mill st. **L** on 14th, 1 block.
R on Trade. **L** on 19th, 1 block.
R on Ferry. **L** on 23rd.

Tours at Mill. #8 M-Sa 10-5

L on State 1/2 block.
R on 21st, 1 block. **L** on Chemeketa.
R on 14th. (site of first mill.)
L on Marion (for 3 mi. option, stay on Marion St. **L** on Summer. See *)
Cross Capitol, turn **R** on Capitol.
L on path along creek, in Veteran's Memorial.
Carefully cross next street.
Stay on path. **R** at next street, Winter.
Cross Church St, go **L**. Cross footbridge on **R**.
Go down Knapp St.
R at corner to read History Marker. Turn around, continue on High St. **L** on Court.
L at Mall corner, **R** on Center, *
R at next corner, on mall.
Cross Court St. to Capitol.

on Knapp St.

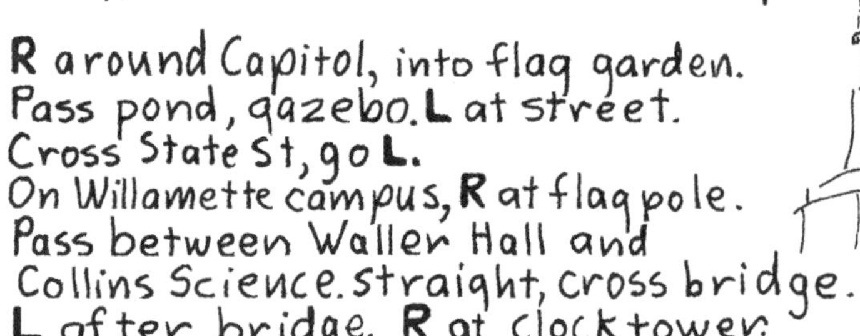

Gold top of Capitol. pioneer figure.

R around Capitol, into flag garden.
Pass pond, gazebo. **L** at street.
Cross State St, go **L**.
On Willamette campus, **R** at flagpole.
Pass between Waller Hall and Collins Science. straight, cross bridge.
L after bridge. **R** at clocktower.
L at Eagles Nest Statue, on sidewalk around lot.
L at street, Pringle. Cross 12th, go **L**. **R** on Mill.

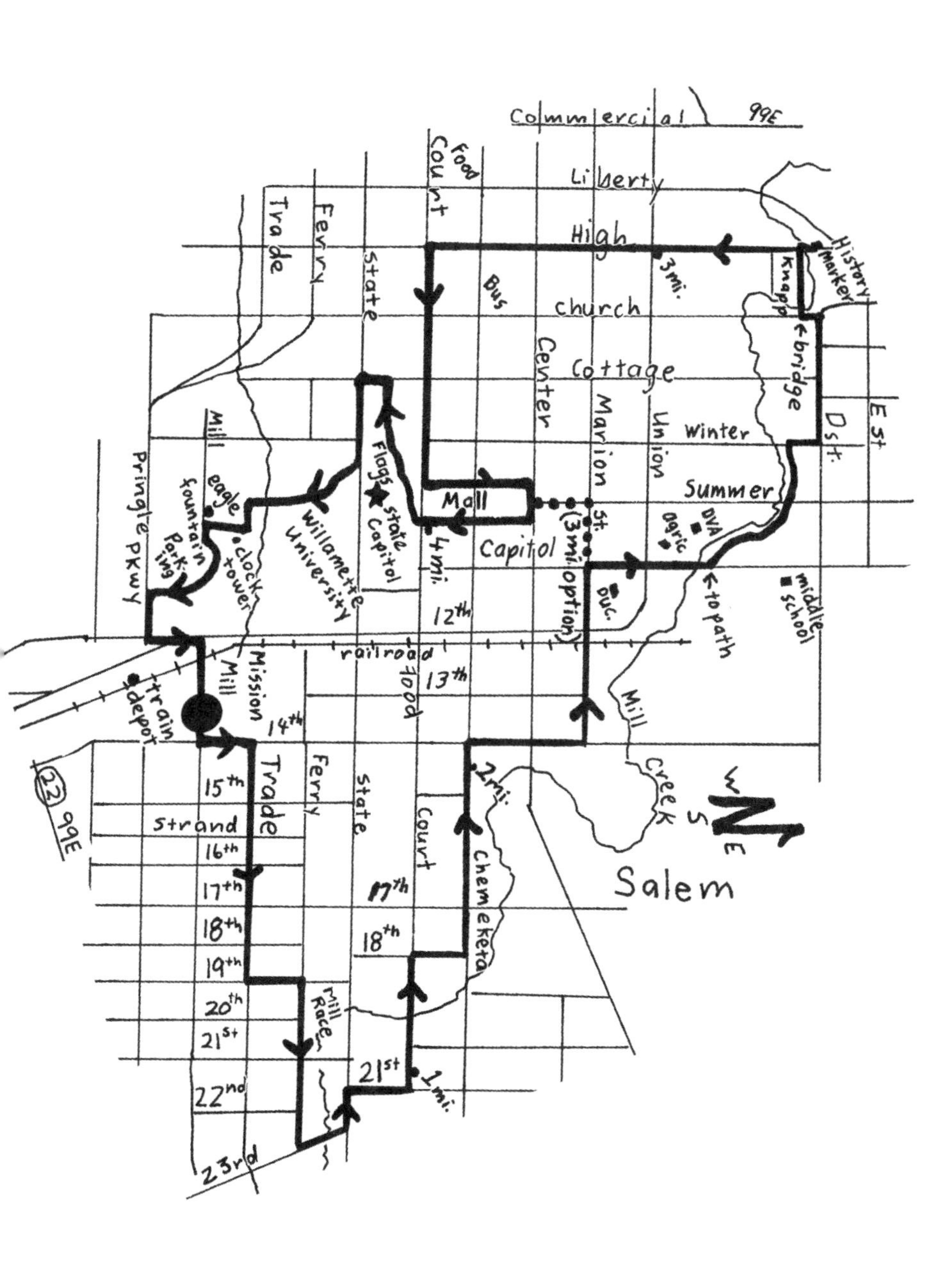
Commercial
99E
Liberty
High
3mi.
History Marker
Knapp
bridge
church
Cottage
Winter
Summer
Court
food court
Ferry
Trade
State
Bus
Center
Marion
Union
D st.
E st
Mall
Flags
state Capitol
4mi.
Capitol
st.
(3mi option)
DVA
agric
DUC.
to path
middle school
Mill
eagle
fountain
Parking
clock tower
Willamette University
Pringle PKWY
12th
railroad
13th
Mill
Mission
14th
Wood
train depot
22
99E
15th
Trade
Ferry
State
Court
2mi.
Strand
16th
17th
18th
19th
20th
21st
22nd
23rd
Chemeketa
Mill Race
1mi.
Mill Creek
Salem

WASHBURNE DISTRICT

Springfield

Distances: 1.2 mi, 2.3 mi. or 3.5 mi. Flat.

Start/finish: So. A st and So. B St./Pioneer Pkwy. W.
Park behind the depot - Sprg. Chamber of Commerce.
Emx bus to bus station from Eugene.

935 B Street
Porch

from parking lot, go **L.** Cross So. 2nd. at corner.
L on S. B to Pioneer Parkway.

Hip roof

River Rock front Porch
407 C street

R on 'A' st.
L on 10th st., 1 block.
L on 'B' st.
(for 1.2 mi, **L** on 4th **R** on Main.
L on Pioneer Pkwy W to end.)

R on 4th, 1 block.
R on 'C' st.
L on 10th st. 1 block.
L on 'D' st.
(for 2.3 mi. **L** on 4th
R on Main **L** on Pioneer Pky to end.)

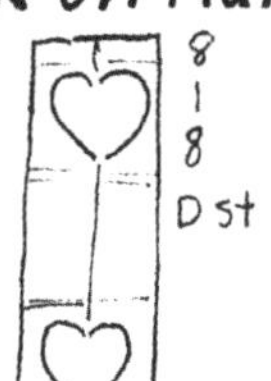
818 D st

R on 4th, 1 block.
R on 'E' st.
L on 10th, 1 block.
L on 'F' st.

R on Main St., 2 blocks.
L on Pioneer Parkway W to end.

Springfield Christian Church

404 C street

Pink and blue "corner" house
1890

Historical information available at
- www.ci.springfield.or.us/dsd/hcommission/washburne.htm.
- Sometimes at the Springfield Chamber of Commerce.

Directions from I-5 to the start:

Coming from the south on I-5.

Exit 189 for 30th Av.
Merge onto Franklin/99.
R on So. 2nd at Pioneer Pkwy W.
Immediate **R** into parking lot of old depot.

Coming from the north on I-5.

Exit 194A toward Springfield.
Merge onto I-105, then 126N.
Exit to Pioneer Parkway.
R on Pioneer Parkway W.
After crossing So. A St,
R into old depot parking lot.

Monkey Tree

EMX bus from Eugene Station, to Springfield Station. Then walk **L** on So. A St, 2 blocks to start.

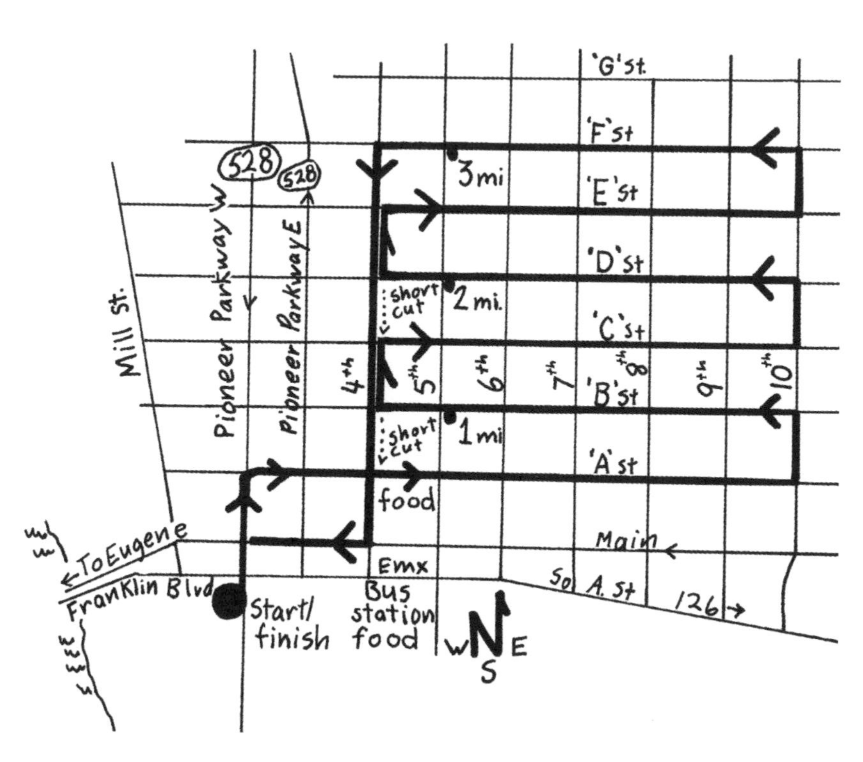

DORRIS RANCH Springfield

Distance: 1.5 mi. flat,* or 4 mi. 126 ft. elevation

Start/finish for 4 mi. walk: So. 'A' st. and Pioneer Parkway, in Parking lot behind the depot, the Spr. Chamber of Commerce.

United States Mail Railway Post Office

From the parking lot, walk to the corner. **R** on So. 'A' St. **R** on 5th. Curve **R** on So 'B' st. to railroad tracks. **L** across street at tracks. Up path on Steps. **R** through old cemetery, around to the street.

R on street 'C' st. for 1/2 block.
L on So. 3rd.
R on 'E' st.
L street, (So. 2nd.)

Tomseth House

Big Maple in meadow.

*for 1.5 mi. walk, park at Dorris Ranch.
Straight into Dorris Ranch.
Pass barn. **R** through green gate.
Trail meanders to river, turns left.

L at the fork. Road ends at orchard.
Go into the orchard.
veer right through trees.
At big maple in meadow,
R on road.
Continue on So. 2nd back to end

filberts

Road Orchard

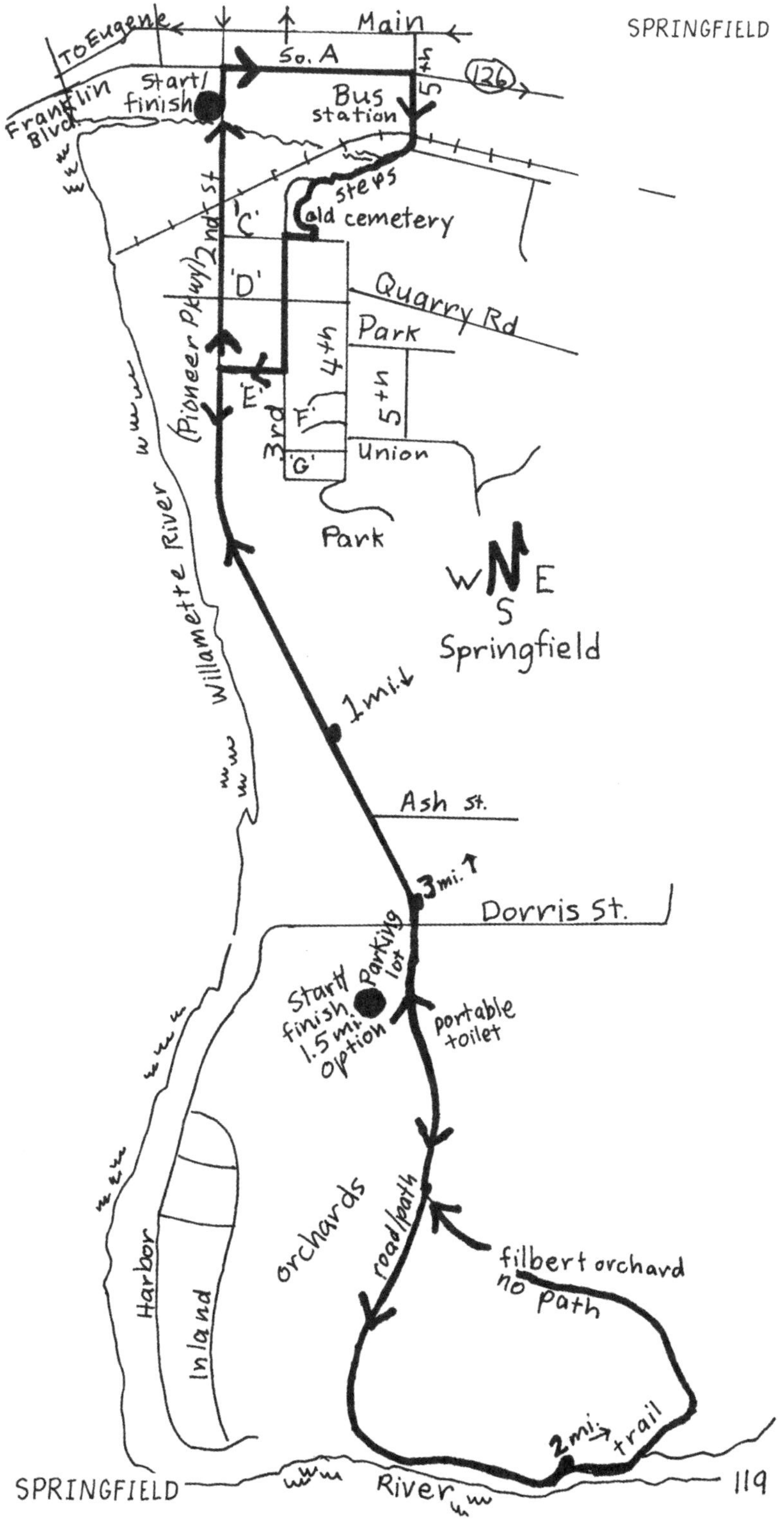

To Eugene
Main
So. A
126
5th
Franklin Blvd.
Start/finish
Bus station
steps
old cemetery
'C'
2nd St
'D'
Quarry Rd
(Pioneer Pkwy)
Park
4th
'E'
'F'
5th
3rd
Union
'G'
Park
W N E
S
Springfield
Willamette River
1 mi.↓
Ash St.
3 mi.↑
Dorris St.
parking lot
Start/finish 1.5 mi. option
portable toilet
orchards
road/path
filbert orchard
no path
Harbor
Inland
2 mi.→
trail
River

KELLY BUTTE Springfield

Distance: 2 mi. flat or 3.5 mi. with 180 ft. elevation

Start/finish: So. 'A' St. and Pioneer Parkway, in the parking lot behind the depot, the Spr. Chamber of Commerce.

With your back to the depot entrance,
Go straight across parking lot.
Veer **R** to pass through arbor.
L after arbor. **R** on path.
Through parking lot.
R into Day Island Park.

Stay on path along river.
Curves **R**, over footbridge
L at street ('D' st.).
L on bike path.
R at fork in path.
R on road (Aspen), 1 block.
Cross street ('D' st). Go **R**.

view of Sisters/Peaks

L on River Hills.
R on Granite.
L on Prescott.
R on Wallace, curves **R** onto Summit.

Sharp **L** into Kelly Butte Park.
L around loop. Pause for the view.
Return to Summit. **L** on Summit.
Cross 'D' St. Go **L**.

R on Water St. onto path over foot bridge. Immediate **L** on path, pass restrooms, playground, under bridges, back to finish.

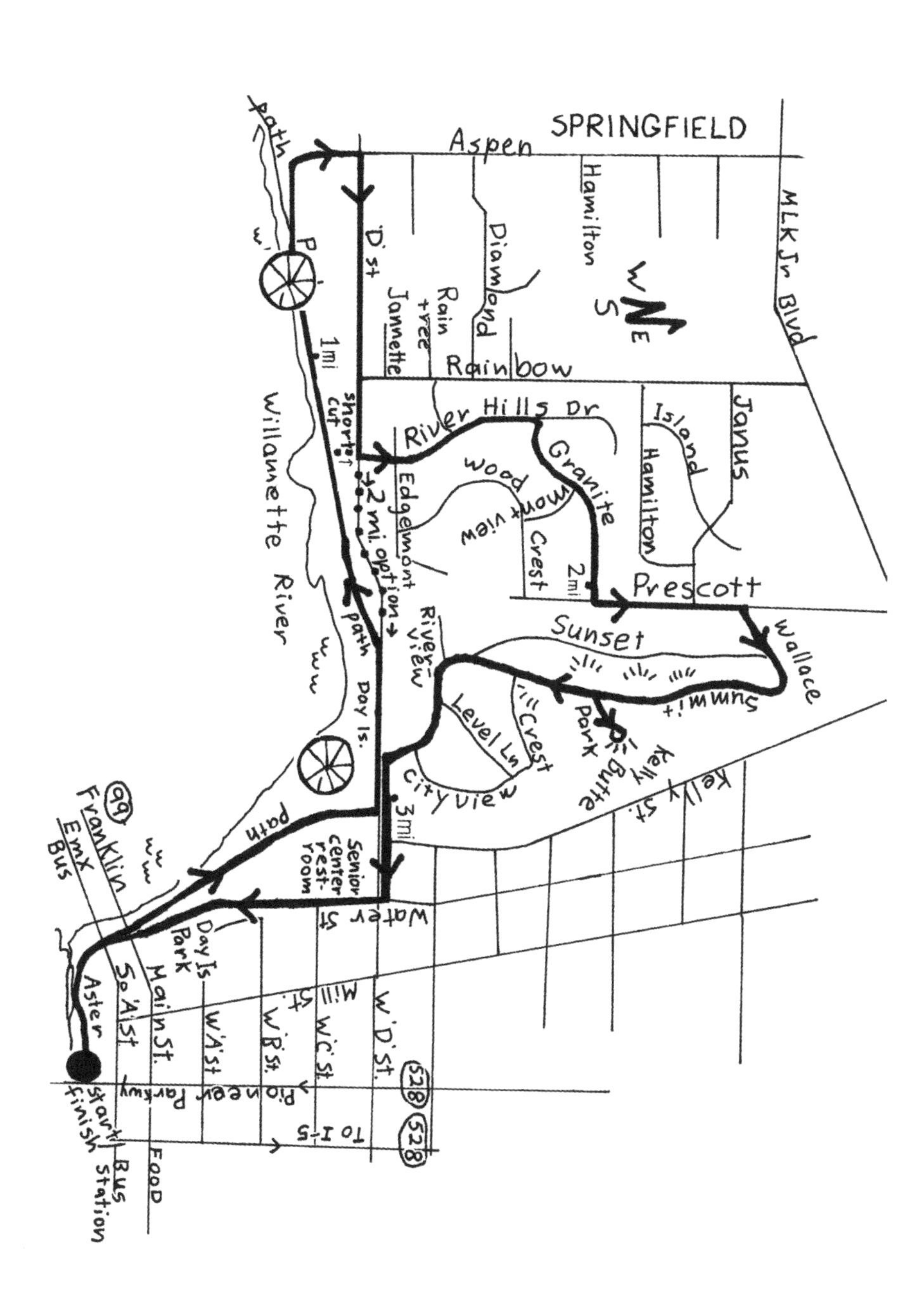

SPRINGFIELD
Aspen
Hamilton
MLK Jr Blvd
Diamond
Rain tree
Jannette
'D' st
Rainbow
path
Willamette River
shortcut
1 mi
River Hills Dr
Granite
Island
Hamilton
Janus
Edgemont
Wood
Mount view
Crest
2 mi
2 mi. option
Prescott
River-view
Sunset
Wallace
path
Day Is.
Summit
Level Ln
Crest
Park
Butte
Kelly St.
City view
3 mi
Senior center rest-room
path
Water St
Franklin
EmX Bus
99
Day Is Park
Aster
So 'A' St
Main St.
W 'A' St
W 'B' St.
W 'C' St
Mill St
W 'D' St.
526
Pioneer Parkwy
To I-5
start/finish
Bus station
Food

SUTHERLIN

Distance: *2 mi. or 4.1 mile. Ascent 124 ft.

From I-5: from north - Exit 140 on to 99, follow signs.
L on W. Central Ave.
from south - Exit 138, toward Sutherlin.
R on W. Central Ave.

R on Willamette to Dean. Park on street by Community center, the start.
With your back to the entry, walk
R on Willamette, 1 block.

NO. 100

L on Central.
R on State.
R on 2nd, 1 block.
L on Umpqua, 1 block.
L on 3rd, 1 block.
R on State, 1 block.
Cross 4th, go **R** on sidewalk.

L up street directly behind school.
(No sign for Willamette St.)
Cross 6th st, go **R**.
R at stop sign, on to Madronna, 1 blk.
*(for 2 mi, **R** on 4th, see * below.)

great mural
Ford
VICK 56
between Fifth and Sixth

L on 4th. **L** up Sherwood.
R on 6th. Pass St. John st.
Road becomes alley, then road.
R down Jade.

view from 6th

***R** on 4th. At school, cross to right to walk on sidewalk.
L on Umtilla, 1 block.
R on 3rd, 1 block.
L on Willamette to end.

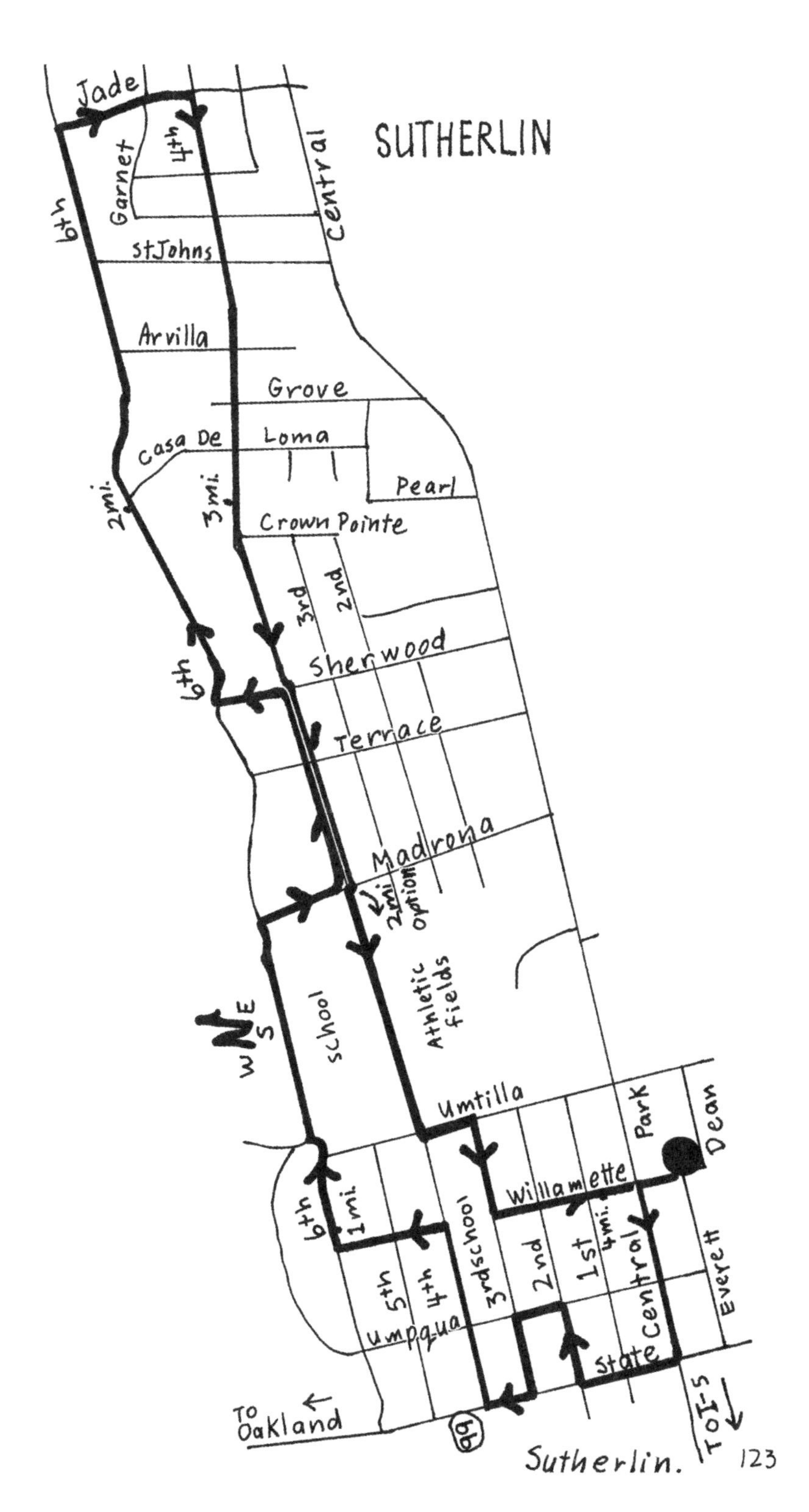
SUTHERLIN
Jade
Garnet
4th
Central
6th
StJohns
Arvilla
Grove
Casa De
Loma
Pearl
2mi.
3mi.
Crown Pointe
3rd
2nd
Sherwood
6th
Terrace
Madrona
2mi option
Athletic fields
school
N
W
E
S
Umtilla
Park
Dean
Willamette
6th
1mi.
4mi.
1st
Central
2nd
3rd
school
5th
4th
Everett
Umpqua
State
To Oakland
99
To I-5
Sutherlin.

Walker's Diary

Town	Route	Date	Notes

Walker's Diary

Town	Route	Date	Notes

Walker's Diary

Town	Route	Date	Notes

Walker's Diary

Town	Route	Date	Notes

About the Author and Illustrator, Tyler E. Burgess

Born in 1950 in the shadow of the Bighorn mountains, I grew up on a cattle ranch near Sheridan, Wyoming. While earning a Business degree at the University of Wyoming, I married, had two children, Sara and Damon. We moved to Billings, Montana, raised the children, divorced and eventually I moved to Eugene, Oregon, where my son was a student.

For athletics, I have always loved outdoor sports. In my 40's I played soccer, did triathlons, multi-sport events, solo backpack trips.

In 2000 I founded Walk With Me, and have coached marathon walking training, taught fitness walking classes at the University of Oregon and Lane Community College.

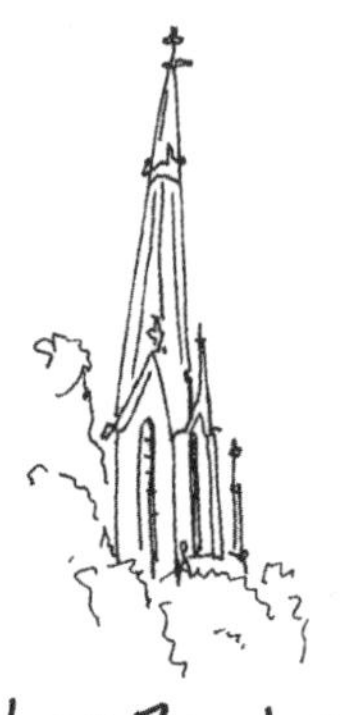

Also I have organized and led walking trips across England, in Ireland, Italy and Morocco. Plus New York City, Boston and Washington DC.

In the fall of 2008 I did a solo walk 550 miles in Spain, the pilgrimage, Way of St. James.

Other Books:
Walking Made Powerful
Eugene, Oregon Walks
How to Walk a Marathon, 26.2 Tips